DIVINE PURPOSE

DIVINE PURPOSE

Published by House of Knowledge
Copyright © 2021 by Joshua M. Raats
All rights reserved

ISBN: 978-0-620-97360-1

Edited by Susan-Jane Redelinghuys
Proofread by Gabrielle Da Silva and Rudolph Du Toit

Unless otherwise stated, scripture quotations are from the NKJV Bible.

DIVINE PURPOSE

by: JOSHUA M. RAATS

HOUSE OF KNOWLEDGE

For my Lord, Jesus Christ.

Contents

Introduction

On a night in April, 2019, I lay awake struggling to fall asleep. It felt as if I were in the middle of a war zone. The windows of my little room seemed to be in the crossfire, with thick raindrops like bullets hitting them continuously. The thunder seemed to land like explosions, shaking the walls and sending me deeper for cover under my blanket. Bright, flashbangs of lightning provided the only moments of visibility in the darkened room. It was a sudden thunderstorm; nature's ambush on the peaceful night. Looking back at that night, it is clear to see the power and presence of God in the storm and I am again reminded that the lifespan of that mighty storm was at the mercy of King Jesus, who just like that night in the boat with His disciples, could at the command of His words have rebuked the storm and restored serenity to the night (Matthew 8:26). He didn't though, and the storm continued to rage all through the night.

To add to the woes of the night was an even more frightening storm. This one did not rattle the roof of my room, but rather raged deep within my heart, shaking the foundations of my soul. The required fortitude to overcome this storm could not be built up through faithful thinking alone. To overcome this storm I would need God Himself to breathe fortitude into my soul. So I opened my Bible and started to read. In so-doing, I inhaled God's breath, which is kept safely housed in each word. After reading for a short while, the storm within me subsided. The only sound that I could hear was from outside: heaven's lullabying melody of thunder, lightning and rain. But, the night was far from over. Early in the morning, I heard God's voice; a tiny whisper from within which so easily could have been mistaken for my own thought. The voice was gentle and clear. "It's time to leave," it said. A sweet melody to my ears. God had spoken.

On the night of the storm, I was staying in a guest house in Bloemfontein, while on a company business trip. Two months prior to the trip I started experiencing intense anxiety and confusion; unable to work a single day without battling those overwhelming feelings which seemed to have developed almost overnight, and which seemed to have no clear source. No matter how hard I tried, I could simply not suppress them. What made these unexpected feelings so much more difficult to understand, was the fact that I was experiencing them, not in a season where I was far from God, but rather during a time when I was walking very closely with the Lord. My life was very much about bringing God glory and the motivation to succeed in my career, which was now causing great distress in my life, was driven by a desire to build God's kingdom through the financial strength that I would be able to offer. But, despite my intentions being for God's glory, they were still very much my intentions. And, although I was indeed walking closely with the Lord and doing the right things, like going to church, reading the Bible and praying, I was actually not listening to God. I was not at an honest place of surrender, willing to obey whatever God asked. Oswald Chambers writes, "....before we choose to follow God's will, a crisis must develop in our lives. This happens because we tend to be unresponsive to God's gentle nudges. He brings us to a place where He asks us to be our utmost for Him and we begin to debate. He then providentially produces a crisis where we have to decide - for or against? That moment becomes a great crossroads in our lives..." It was through the emotional storm of anxiety and confusion that God eventually led me to that crossroad. He told me that He does not want my sacrifices, but rather my obedience. Stepping out in faith, I chose to surrender my life to God, and be boldly obedient to whatever He asked. Although God had told me that night in Bloemfontein that it was time for me to quit my job, I would soon discover that our understanding of the word time differs significantly - my understanding was that it meant now, and His understanding was that it meant whenever He decided. For it would be another nine months before I would eventually end up leaving the company. Those nine months birthed in me a bold obedience and trust that allowed me to completely surrender to God's will. In that time God would ask me to do something, and I would be faced with the choice of either trusting in Him and obeying, or trusting in my own understanding and essentially rebelling. The decisions were never easy to make and on many occasions I was tempted to make the wrong decision, simply out of fear. But, with the help of God's wisdom and the council of those around me, I continued to make the decisions of obedience. After every obedient decision made, God proved faithful, blessing my life in some way or another because of it.

Three months after the stormy night in Bloemfontein and while I was still working for the company, God spoke again. This time, He told me to move 40km from where I was currently staying, to a house in the Cape Winelands town of Stellenbosch. He told me I was to stay there for only three months. It was during this time when the move out of my career really started to take shape. I was about halfway into my stay when God started to press into my heart the idea of a career in the wine industry, in particular, grape farming and wine making. With that new desire, which I believed to be from God, I contacted a friend of mine, Jasper Raats, who is a well-established wine farmer in the area, to find out more about the industry. After a few conversations, which I believe were divinely led by the Holy Spirit, it became clear to me that God was opening a door for me to start a career in the wine industry. Eventually that door was flung wide open and Jasper offered me an opportunity to work for him. The details of the opportunity were very vague, but essentially consisted of the following: I could work on the farm in Stellenbosch during the two month harvest period, assisting wherever there was a need. In the process, I could learn as much as possible about grape farming and wine making from him. The work would be very labor intensive and I would be paid the national minimum wage for each hour worked. There would be no official job contract and there would be no benefits such as medical aid or a retirement policy. Basically, the opportunity meant that I was to quit my job in corporate, give up financial security and the possibility of a very lucrative career, and go and work on a farm in Stellenbosch. It was a daunting prospect, but I knew that it was God who had opened this door for me and I knew that it was God asking me to be obedient to Him yet again. But when I began to consider the financial implications of such a decision, reason started to cloud my faith. For it seemed financially impossible that this could work. Since my three months stay in Stellenbosch was over and I had already moved back home from Stellenbosch when Jasper made me the offer, I would have to rent another place should I accept the offer. But since the salary offered was so low, I would not be able to rent a home in Stellenbosch. Instead, I would have to travel 80km to and from the farm every day, and my daily wage would barely be able to cover the cost of fuel for the journey. There was no logical or rational explanation for choosing to take the offer, but a deep-rooted conviction that God was taking me on a journey, built on absolute obedience to His will, made me confident that resigning from my corporate job and accepting the offer to work on the farm, was the right decision. After taking advice from council, and having received the peace I needed from God, I resigned from my corporate job and accepted the job on the farm.

Shortly before I was to start working on the farm, Jasper told me that I could stay with Huey Van Rensburg, the farm manager on the estate. The Van Rensburg family provided me with free accommodation, and arranged lunch for me during the day and dinner for me each evening. Their hospitality and generosity allowed God to use them as vessels for His blessing to me. God had shown His faithfulness to my obedience yet again by removing all the financial obstacles. A few days before my first day of work on the farm, the phrase *divine purpose* filled my mind for the first time. I considered for some time what it might mean, but nothing came to mind. I wrote it down and then asked the Lord to reveal to me what it meant, if it was indeed from Him.

I was three weeks into the harvest and the cellar was extremely busy on this particular day: forklifts were moving in and out, bringing grapes in that had just arrived on trucks. Pressing machines were hard at work squeezing all the juice out of the grapes and the conveyor belt on the sorting machine was being loaded with what seemed like an endless supply of grapes. It was in all this chaos that I heard Jasper shout, with a sense of urgency, to someone else across the cellar, "We need to get the grapes in! That is the most important thing to do!" As he said that, the Holy Spirit whispered to me, "Look how much effort people are putting in to bring these grapes into the cellar. How much more does your Heavenly Father not want His children to come home." Later that afternoon, while I was in the vineyard, I felt surrounded by God's presence and I heard the Holy Spirit tell me, "divine purpose". I knew God was trying to tell me something. And then, just like that night in Bloemfontein all those months ago, I heard that tiny whisper again: gentle and clear, "I want you to write a book, and it will be called Divine Purpose". One week later, I left the farm, ready for the next step of my journey with God.

The process of writing this book has been wonderful and I have come to know more of God's faithfulness through writing it. Each day before I sat down to write, I committed my writing to God and asked the Holy Spirit to lead me in everything that I wrote. The words to follow are inspired by God and contain God's intended message for you. I have merely been given the honour to write His words down. All the good that may come out of this book for your life, is because of God. All the glory belongs to Him. My hope for you in reading this book is twofold: Firstly, that you will be encouraged by the knowledge that God truly can and does use anybody to do His work for His Kingdom. 1 Corinthians 2:9 says, "Eye has not seen, nor ear heard, nor have entered into heart of man the things which God has prepared for those who love Him." God has beautiful plans. All you need to do is surrender to God and be boldly obedient to what He asks of you. When my fiancé Gaby and I had just started to get to know each other, before we were even dating, she wrote me a letter which concluded with the following words, "Be brave and very courageous Josh, and your life will be better than any world, in any book you've ever read. God is the greatest Author." I hope that this book will encourage you to have the bravery and courage to always stay close to

Jesus Christ and to let Him write your story for you. Secondly, my hope is that you will read this book with an open and expectant heart, confident that your Maker can encourage you with the words you need in every season you find yourself in and that you will be reminded that God is always with you, lovingly guiding you along the path of faithfulness. This path is narrow, and on occasion, feels far from God, but it has a glorious end destination. Along the way He will surprise you with the awareness of His presence, providing you with all the strength and hope you need, to serve Him and ultimately enter into the Kingdom of heaven.

Prologue

In Genesis 2:8, Moses tells us how "The Lord God planted a garden...and there He put the man who He had formed." God's hope was for Man to tend to the garden so that it would yield fruit as an offering to Him. But man failed, and the garden became a desolate place that yielded no fruit, but only thorns and thistles (Genesis 3:18). Four thousand years later, and God's story of redemption also unfolds in a garden. This time, instead of bringing a man called Adam forth from the ground, another man Jesus, would be sent to the ground. A few days before this man Jesus would be sent to the ground, He told His disciples that, "unless a grain of wheat falls into the ground and dies, it remains alone, but if it dies it produces much fruit" (John 12:24). With these words Jesus revealed how His death on the cross, and burial in this garden, would be like a seed that is sown in the ground. This meant that Jesus' body would be the first seed sown in His Father's new garden. Three days later Jesus, in His resurrected state, became the first fruit of that new garden. In this new garden, God would not leave the fate of its fruit in the hands of man again, but rather He would give the responsibility of tending the entire garden

7

to His Son, Jesus Christ (Ephesians 1:22). In John 20:15 when Mary saw the resurrected Jesus and "supposed Him to be the gardener", this was no mistake, but rather a prophetic identification of who Jesus was to be. Jesus was not only the resurrected first fruit of the garden, but He was also to be the Gardener, responsible for supplying everything that is needed, so that all other fruit of the garden will grow and increase (2 Corinthians 9:10) to His likeness.

Enclosed in the walls of this beautiful new garden, we find a vineyard. The prophet Isaiah sang, "My Well-beloved has a vineyard on a very fruitful hill. He dug it up and cleared out its stones, and planted it with the choicest vine." This vineyard did not suddenly appear in the garden. To get there, it required somebody to make a sacrifice and to do labour, for "ground had to be dug up and stones had to be moved". The labourer is the Gardener, Jesus Christ, and His sacrifice is found on a hill at the cross, and in the stripes on His back, the holes in His hands, and the scar on His side. But it was not for an actual vineyard that Jesus would endure this labour, for the prophet Isaiah is not singing of an actual vineyard but rather using a vineyard as an analogy to refer to God's people. (Isaiah 5:7). We can, therefore, rejoice in song with the prophet Isaiah knowing that we are God's vineyard; intentionally planted and under the meticulous care of Jesus Christ the Gardener, who endured the brutal labour of the cross so that we would have a space in His Father's garden.

In Genesis 8:22 God made a promise, one which holds true in His new garden too, that "while the earth remains, seedtime and harvest, cold and heat, winter and summer, and day and night shall not cease." And since that promise was made, God's vineyard has never failed to experience the seasons. Each season visits the vineyard just to be chased away by the next season; a perpetual cycle that obeys no man, but only yields to God's will. The only certainty is its paradoxical ebb and flow: cold comes before heat, winter comes before summer, day comes before night. In God's vineyard no season is stable and change, though mysterious, is sure. Though it may appear as a random system governed by chance, there is a perfect God-designed order in the vineyard which works all things together for the good according to God's purpose (Romans 8:28).

Charles H. Spurgeon said in a sermon preached in 1886 that, "Holy Scripture is intended not to teach us natural but spiritual things." The intention of this book, therefore, is not to teach us about the natural principles of the vineyard, but rather it is to use the Biblical illustrations of Jesus Christ as the Gardener, the Christian life as the vineyard and the God created and God-governed principles of the seasons, as analogies to deduce spiritual conclusions relevant to the Christian life. And it is then, on top of those spiritual conclusions, that we will confidently and securely answer the complex question, "What is my Divine Purpose?".

DIVINE PURPOSE

Chapter 1

Autumn

Once a year the earth becomes a canvas which God paints with rich colours of yellow, red, purple, gold and orange. A time where God, with gentle brush strokes reveals the glorious yet fading beauty of His Autumn. A season that connects the past with the future, a transition between what once was and what is to be; a golden-brown bridge that creeks to the sound of crunching leaves and that provides a path from Summer to Winter. This transition that happens in Autumn is especially true, and essential in a vineyard. Without the Autumn bridge between Summer and Winter, the vineyard would not be able to adapt to the sudden change in weather that comes with Winter. Autumn is the beautiful transition that gently leads the vineyard in preparation for what awaits in Winter. The process by which this all takes place and which I will briefly explain, follows three principles of nature. Firstly, the winds begin to change. Secondly, the leaves of the vineyard begin to dull. And finally, these leaves fall off the branch. Each one of these principles is supported by well-studied and in-depth biological explanations. However, the aim of this chapter only requires that we have a basic understanding of each principle, and therefore I will side-step the bulk of the biological explanation and provide rather a brief and simple explanation that we can use as context to reach further conclusions. Before we get to the three natural principles, it will serve us well to remember that the pages to follow are in no way intended to teach us about the natural principles of the vineyard during Autumn. But rather, under the guidance of God's wisdom and the truth of His Holy Scripture, we will use those natural principles as the foundational context to deduce three spiritual conclusions relevant to the Christian life, keeping in mind that God governs all the seasons, and that the vineyard and the Gardener are Biblical illustrations representing the Christian life and Jesus, respectively.

The Winds Begin to Change

The first natural principle is found in the arrival of a disruptive wind. As Autumn settles-in in the vineyard, it brings with it a rather unpleasant guest- the disruptive wind, whose previous visit has all but been forgotten after the pleasant summer months. As soon as this unexpected guest arrives, life in the vineyard starts to become a lot less comfortable than it was in Summer. The wind spends its days running between the vineyard rows kicking up soil and grass which lands like explosive debris on, what used to be, clean green leaves, leaving behind a trail of disarray on the vineyard floor. The familiar vineyard sounds: the busy buzzing of the bees and the chirpy chatter of the swallows, start to become drowned out by the wind's frequent tantrums. On some days the wind is so severe that the vineyard leaves are forced to close their stomata (the little openings on their surface responsible for exchanging air with the atmosphere). When they close their stomata, the leaves are unable to properly breathe and consequently struggle to produce food. This troublesome wind also pulls the clouds in and over the vineyard, blocking out the sunshine and causing a sudden chill to fill the vineyard. This Autumn wind is an unpleasant and unseen force, yet a force of nature that God commands and has His eyes on at all times. A divine force which, as the vineyard has always experienced, plays an undeniably important role in the long term growth and well-being of the vineyard.

The Leaves of the Vineyard Begin to Dull

The second natural principle is found in the colour of the leaves which begin to dull. Every leaf in the vineyard has tiny structures called chloroplasts, which are filled with a substance called chlorophyll (for clarity we can say that the chloroplast is the factory and the chlorophyll is the fuel that the factory uses). The chlorophyll has the ability to absorb sunlight which is then used as the energy to convert carbon dioxide and water into food for the leaf. Chlorophyll contains the strong green pigment that gives the leaf its bright green colour, but during Autumn two processes take place which will eventually dull all the green in the leaves. Firstly, as the wind starts bringing in more clouds above the vineyard, the temperature in the vineyard begins to drop. Secondly, the days start to become shorter, decreasing the amount of sunlight available to the leaves. As a result of these unfavourable conditions, the chloroplast shuts down the food-making process as a way to conserve energy. And, since no food is being produced, the chlorophyll is no longer needed and begins to break down and disappear, removing the bright green colour from the leaf. As the chlorophyll disappears, other substances try to get a quick chance at revealing their pigments before the leaves eventually fall off the branch. As a result, we see the bright green vineyard leaves change into dull shades of yellow, red and even purple.

The Leaves Fall off the Branch

The third and final natural principle is the falling of the dull leaves from the branch. For a long while, despite their dullness, the leaves remain quite safely attached to the branch. However, for a while already the cells on the branch have slowly been pushing the leaves away, weakening their connection to the branch until they eventually fall to the ground. This needs to happen in order for the branch to survive the heavy rain that Winter brings.

Before we explore the spiritual conclusions relevant in each of the three natural principles, we must first understand that a transition season like Autumn is as real and as necessary in a Christian life as it is in a vineyard. Just like Summer doesn't last forever in a vineyard, Jesus doesn't promise us an endless Summer from the moment we choose to follow Him. Jesus even asked us to "count the cost" (Luke 14:28) and make sure that we understand that following Him is by no means a matter of constant Summer. Therefore "do not think it strange concerning the fiery trial which is to try you, as though some strange thing has happened to you..." (1 Peter 4:12). However, you can rest in the knowledge that God is intentional in taking you through this season and that if He has begun a transition, then "...He who has begun a good work in you will complete it..." (Philippians 1:6).

Spiritual Conclusion 1

The first spiritual conclusion is found in the wind. If God has led you into a transition phase, you may begin to experience slight changes in your environment; subtle disruptions caused by a force which you cannot directly see nor define, a force like the wind whose presence is felt only if exerted upon you. And, if exerted upon you, it is felt as a disturbance to your everyday comforts. Instead of the actual impact of the force, it is rather the knowledge that this force is out of our control, which has us crying out like the disciples in the boat: "Master, Master, we are perishing!" (Luke 8:24). However, for the disciples it was at their moment of deepest distress that Jesus "...rebuked the wind...and there was a calm" (Luke 8:24) and the disciples see for the first time that even the uncontrollable force that is creating distress in their lives, is being controlled by Jesus (Luke 8:25). But God's sovereignty over this disruptive wind is even greater than just commanding it, for He also "creates the wind" (Amos 4:13) and "causes His wind to blow" (Psalm 147:18). Every aspect of the disruptive force that you may be experiencing, is controlled by God. He has determined the strength, the sound and the duration of its gusts. And He has done so knowing full well what you will be able to endure if you rely on Him to get you through the storm (1 Corinthians 10:13). Although we do not know from which side the wind will blow tomorrow (John 3:8), we can have confidence that God does know, for His ways and His thoughts are higher than ours (Isaiah 55:9). So, we should therefore not be afraid to rejoice when the wind starts to blow in our lives and disrupts our comfort, for it was the winds that blew across the Shulamite's garden that caused its spices to flow out (Song of Solomon 4:16). It was also the strong east wind that, as Spurgeon writes, "cast Paul shipwrecked, naked and forlorn, upon the Rock of Ages", and ultimately it is the wind of God that blows away the chaff of our life (Psalm 1:4) - that worthless debris that so often piles up in our lives and takes up space God intends to occupy.

Spiritual Conclusion 2

The second spiritual conclusion is found in the dulling of the colour in the leaves which, in the Christian life, refers to a dulling of our spiritual comforts. In John 15:5, Jesus says, "I am the vine and you are the branches. He who abides in me, and I in him, bears much fruit; for without me you can do nothing." We must also remember from earlier that although Jesus is the Gardener of this vineyard, He is also "the resurrected first fruit", hence the original vine from which all branches grow and from which all fruit will come forth. If Jesus is the vine and we are the branches, we must then identify the leaves in our lives. Our leaves are the things which come from God and which accentuate our spiritual life and our pursuit of God. They are the things which we can't look at without considering that God must have been involved in providing them. They are our spiritual comforts: the feelings we experience as a result of being in God's presence. These feelings reflect God's characteristics and are dependent on the extent to which God reveals Himself to us. For lack of a better description, they are the residue of God's nature that sticks to us during, and for a while after we have been in His presence. The fullness of joy that we find in His presence (Psalm 16:11) and the peace that comes with God lifting His countenance upon us (Numbers 6:26), are feelings which God can choose to bless us with while we are in His presence. What we cannot afford to miss though, is that they bring comfort to our lives which takes us from the valley to the mountain top. Even though we glorify God when we are on top of the mountain, we must never forget that the Christian life is not only about experiencing God on the mountain top, but also about knowing that God is with us in the valley. For as wonderful as these Godly experiences are, if we keep looking to them as the standard product of our faith, then soon enough they become like bright green leaves that we look to for assurance that our faith in Jesus is real and justifiable. And looking for assurance of God in this way is building the wrong kind of faith. It creates a faith in your faith, instead of a faith in God. It incorrectly measures our faith based on what we experience emotionally with God and what we see physically from God, as opposed to what we believe about who God is. But the Bible says that "We walk by faith and not by sight"(2 Corinthians 5:7) and therefore we should not rely on feelings and experiences to feed our faith because they are temporary. That is why the branch can't look to the greenness of the leaves for assurance of the vine, because the leaves aren't always going to be green. The branch needs to face the vine. Similarly, we need to keep our eyes fixed on Jesus and not on what He does for us. We should acknowledge what He does for us and give Him thanks for it, but our faith should not be in what He does, but rather in who He is. For "faith is the substance of things hoped for and the evidence of things unseen" (Hebrews 11:1), which means our faith is not in the experiential moments of Holy awareness, but rather in the things we cannot yet see and in what we expect Jesus to do in the future. Consequently, God may need to dull these comforts so that we will build our faith on the unseen person of Jesus, as opposed to the seen things that He does for us. This process of dulling will not always be easy. It may mean that some days aren't filled with the joy that you once knew, or that your quiet time with God feels distant from Him. Whatever it is that God may be dulling in this season, know this: if you have been living righteously and obeying God's word, then this dulling may be a blessing from God which will strengthen your faith in the person of Jesus instead of the experience of Jesus. And in this season, no matter how dull the days may be, do not charge God with wrong, for "The Lord gave, and the Lord has taken away; blessed be the name of the Lord" (Job 1:21) for "we know that all things work together for good to the ones who love God" (Romans 8:28).

Spiritual Conclusion 3

The third and final spiritual conclusion of Autumn is found in the leaves that fall from the branch. This refers to the temporary removal of our spiritual comforts. This removal takes place only after our spiritual comforts have been dulled to the extent that we have shifted our gaze from the experience of those comforts to the source of those comforts, Jesus - that is a shift from the leaves to the vine. Once our gaze is fixed on Jesus Himself to affirm our faith, and we no longer seek the assurance from the spiritual comforts in our lives, God can remove these leaves of comfort entirely so that the only thing that remains is us and Him - that is, the branch and the vine. This ensures that we have no distractions that may interfere with our focus as God guides us to become entirely dependent on Jesus. It is in this state that we become not just fully dependent on Jesus for everything, but that we become aware of our dependence, and also aware of His provision in satisfying that dependence. It is during this state, where we are fully dependent on Jesus, that we begin to understand and gain confidence that "...in Him we live and move and have our being..." (Acts 17:28). It is also in this state, which is established in Autumn, but which is tried in Winter, where we will discover that having looked to our spiritual comforts for assurance of our faith, was actually a faithless act. It is in Jesus alone where the true substance of what we looked for through experiences is actually found. We will start to believe even more boldly that, although all of our spiritual comforts may have been stripped from us, they are always still available and found in Jesus, whether we experience them or not. It will be this understanding, gained in Winter, which will build a faith in the Lord Jesus. A faith that will be found steadfast and patient under any circumstance, if your life is indeed hidden with Christ in God (Colossians 3:3).

We must, however, understand that the stripping of our leaves of comfort takes place in two ways. One is when the Lord Himself strips you of your leaves of comfort in order to strengthen your faith by teaching you to have your faith in the person of Jesus and not in the experiences of Jesus. This can happen, and often does, while you are living in a way that is pleasing to the Lord and actively engaged in seeking the Lord. This way is a blessing from God, and if you abide in Him as He takes you through it, it will result in you having a stronger faith in Him because of it. The second way is when Christians lose their leaves because they have drifted from God and have started to live a sinful life again. If you recognize that your leaves have been stripped by God as a way for Him to increase your faith, because you have been living obediently in accordance with His statutes, then take heart, for God is doing something good in your life. However, if you believe that your leaves have been stripped because of your sin, and you recognize that you have not been living in obedience to God's statutes, then I would like to offer you comfort, the comfort of Jesus Christ; a comfort that offers you a lifeline of grace that you may reach out to as an escape from the perils of your sin, so that you may once again walk in fellowship with the Lord you once knew so dearly. Therefore let me remind you of the day that Jesus offered you eternal life. Let me remind you of the day that you accepted His death on the cross as the perfect atonement for your sins. And, let me remind you of our God who is rich in mercy, a God who loves you greatly and a God who, when you were dead in your sin, made you alive together with Christ (Ephesians 2:4-5). For although everything around you may have died, your spirit is not dead nor is it dying, for Jesus is still the substance within you that gives you life. And, if you feel that you no longer have faith in Jesus and you can no longer remember the joys of fellowship with Jesus, and you seem to be surrounded by thick clouds of guilt and shame, let me remind you also that He remains faithful even when you are faithless, for God cannot deny Himself (2 Timothy 2:13). Therefore, hold on to the promise of His faithfulness and remember that He is the same God who offered you forgiveness the first time (Hebrews 13:8) and He once again offers that forgiveness to you. So turn from where you are and run back to the Lord, tell Him of your sorrows and ask Him for forgiveness for turning away from Him. Allow Him to restore to you the lush leaves you once had on your branches, and allow Him to restore to you the joy of His salvation (Psalm 51:12), for there is always hope for the Christian who has Jesus Christ alive within them.

I would now like to address the church and others who are spiritually equipped by God to minister restoration to our brothers and sisters who have lost their way and find themselves stripped of their leaves and bound by sin. For to some there is a responsibility given that says, "if a man is overtaken in any trespass, you who are spiritual restore such a one in a spirit of gentleness, considering yourself lest you also be tempted" (Galatians 6:1). The original Greek word used for "restore" is katartizo, and it was used to describe the process of setting broken bones and for fixing broken nets. Both tasks are not easy to carry out and will have negative consequences if not carried out with diligence. For the one who has the broken bone incorrectly set, he may never move properly again, and for the one with a poorly-fixed fishing net, he may never adequately feed his family again. For the Biblical writer to have used that particular meaning of the word "restore" suggests that the responsibility of Christian restoration is immense. And yet, as immense as the responsibility is, it is one given to us by Jesus Christ. We know this because of what we read in John 11:44 about what happened at the tomb of Lazarus; Jesus performed a miracle and raised Lazarus from the dead, but what we see is Lazarus walking out of the tomb still "bound hand and foot with gravecloths and his face was wrapped with a cloth." Although Jesus had raised Lazarus from the dead, there was still a lot that needed to be removed in order for him to walk freely. Restoration needed to take place. Knowing this, Jesus entrusted that restoration to His disciples and told them to "loose him and let him go"(John

11:44). Jesus started the miracle with the resurrection, but then He entrusted the completion of the miracle to His disciples. And so it is the same for our brothers and sisters who have lost their way and find themselves bound by sin and surrounded by bare branches: Jesus performs the first part of their miracle by the instant forgiveness and justification of their sins, a moment of absolute love and grace. But have we, who God has entrusted to complete the miracle, failed in our responsibility? Have we forgotten about discipling and about helping young Christians break old habits? Have we forgotten about teaching young Christians in righteous living and about holding them accountable for their continuance in faith? Have we forgotten about pointing them in the direction of the author and finisher of their faith Jesus Christ (Hebrews 12:2)? Did we stop working once we saw that God had raised them from the dead? Have we made getting people to church so that they will be saved the pinnacle objective of our mission? Do we count the number of saved souls as a measure of our accountability to disciple, or do we count souls in an impossible attempt to measure God's grace? Oswald Chambers wrote, "Our work is not to save souls, but to disciple them. Salvation and sanctification are the work of God's sovereign grace, and our work as His disciples is to disciple others' lives so that they are totally yielded to God." If we have so many Christian brothers and sisters who seem to be losing their leaves and becoming bare branches because of their sin, we need to ask ourselves if we are living up to our God-given responsibility to disciple (Matthew 28:19). We need to understand, again, that our primary work as Christians only starts after God has saved a soul, not before. We do not work towards Sunday; we work from Sunday. God raises them from the dead on Sunday, and we remove their grave-cloth in the week. If we do not live up to this responsibility to disciple newly-saved Christians, we may see many more Christians who walked fully awakened by the grace and power of God, slowly start to fall asleep and begin to wander aimlessly and without purpose on the glorious path of faithfulness, a path that God has intended for them to walk with a confidence and a zeal for His name.

Practical Applications

Autumn is often a difficult, possibly even the most difficult, season for a young (young in spiritual maturity) Christian to experience. It is a season when unexpected and disruptive changes begin to take place in our comfortable and happy Christian life. It is a season when our comfortable feelings of joy and peace begin to dull, and we are left having to remain faithful without always experiencing the comfortable feelings or experiences of our faith. And finally, Autumn is a season when our comfort is removed entirely, when life becomes difficult, and when our faith can no longer be built on our emotions, but only on the person of Jesus Christ. If you find yourself in this season where you have the liberty and joy that comes from giving your life to Christ, only to find the range of that liberty shrinking and your joy fading, do not attempt to reason the matter out on your own and do not panic over this change. Instead, seek the comfort of a loving church community and the wisdom of spiritual elders. Allow these people to lead you to Jesus so that He Himself can explain to you what the cause for this change may be. Allow Him to be the one who assures you that He is with you, despite what is happening. For He *is* with you, and He is guiding you along the path of faithfulness toward your sanctification which He purchased for you by His blood that He shed on the cross.

By considering the spiritual conclusions that we have deduced from the changing of the winds, the dulling of the leaves and the falling of the leaves from the branch, we can conclude by saying: just like Autumn in the vineyard has left the branch entirely bare and revealed to us its dependence on the vine, so too can God take us Christians through a season of transition which reveals to us our dependence on Jesus Christ. God knows that the only way that we will endure the upcoming Winter is if we will abide in Jesus. For it is through abiding in Jesus Christ that we are transformed from having an experiential, self-assured faith to having a steadfast God dependent faith. And it is only the latter kind which will enable us to endure the trials and tribulations of the upcoming Winter months.

Chapter 2

Winter

The Autumn bridge of transition has been crossed- a journey stating intent to remain faithful to Jesus Christ- and one which, despite the very many temptations to turn back, has brought you closer to where Jesus is leading you. Now you are in Winter: a cold, dark and mostly silent season, where the chill from the wet ground seems to chase away any warmth sent down from the sun, where the sun seems to spend most days locked behind thick doors of grey clouds and most of the night hiding behind large black curtains. It is a time when even the singing birds have left, leaving the days filled with echoes of silence, interrupted only by the whimpering gust of the wind and sobbing rain of the clouds. But, despite the obvious negative aspects of Winter, God has not left nature in a terrible state after all. For it is in the hidden, often undiscovered places which our natural eye cannot always see, where God has stored His Winter treasure. It is the cold, wet ground that allows the roots to absorb more water than at any other time of the year. It is the cold air, which holds less moisture, making the night sky more transparent and therefore revealing the true brightness of God's stars. It is only once we discover the treasure that God has hidden in Winter, that we will truly appreciate the often misunderstood cold, dark and silent season. Our treasure expedition will take us to the vineyard, where we will see two natural principles (one being natural in its divine nature and the other inevitable and normal to find it in a vineyard during Winter) which govern and sustain the vineyard during Winter. The first principle is Dormancy (natural in its divine nature) and the second principle is Pruning (natural in its inevitable nature). I will use these natural principles as the context to reveal two spiritual conclusions that are relevant to a Christian, who, like the vineyard, may be experiencing a Winter season.

Dormancy

The first natural principle is dormancy, a phase in Winter during which all physiological activity in the vineyard seems to stop entirely. The vineyard is unable to convert any of its surrounding resources into nutrients and survives on only a small amount of reserve nutrients left over from Autumn, so no growth takes place. To the untrained eye, the vineyard appears to be dead. However, dormancy is the phase in which the vineyard is hibernating; waiting until the conditions become favourable to support the growth of a new bud. Dormancy is necessary to ensure that the bud from which the fruit will eventually develop, does not form too soon and rather forms only when the conditions are perfectly suitable for the new fruit to grow in. By inhibiting the growth of the bud, the plant prevents "bud-break": the process whereby the buds start to swell until eventually breaking open into the new leaf shoots. If bud-break were to happen in the harsh conditions of Winter, the fragile new shoot would not be able to survive, no flower would form and no fruit would be produced. At this stage, we must again be reminded that all principles of nature are God's principles. For "by Him all things were created, in heaven and on Earth, visible and invisible..." (Colossians 1:16). And, we must also be reminded that every one of these principles of nature is also perfect; never flawed and lacking in nothing, for "... His way is perfect, the word of the Lord is flawless..." (Psalm 18:30). We can confidently accept that the process of taking the vineyard through a state of dormancy, is a process that God uses to bring about rapid growth, vitality, and an abundance of nourishment, at precisely the right time.

Pruning

The second natural principle that we find in the vineyard during Winter is pruning. Pruning is the very technical and often rigorous process whereby the gardener of the vineyard will cut away all parts of the branch that will not bear fruit. Pruning has been a perpetual inclusion in the calendar of every vineyard gardener since the start of vineyard farming, which spans thousands of years. By cutting away the dead wood and damaged parts of the branch, the gardener prevents any bacteria from entering the branch and in so doing ensures that the productive parts of the branch will still produce the fruit that he expects. The gardener also prunes branches that have grown too long. Being too far from the vine, they are unable to draw on the structural support that the vine offers, and therefore cannot maintain the weight of any fruit that they would bring forth. The gardener, therefore, cuts these branches shorter so that they are closer to the vine, which will support the weight of the fruit that the branches will bear. As simple as these two pruning processes are to explain, they are far more difficult to execute. In fact, they can only be successfully executed by a knowledgeable gardener who is intentional in ensuring that the owner of the vineyard receives the best quality fruit that the branches can possibly yield.

Having laid the foundation of natural principles, we are nearly ready to start deducing the spiritual conclusions found in each. But before we do that, it will serve us well to remember the analogies that we are carrying with us throughout this book. The Gardener, whom we have seen is the most important person to ensure that pruning is successful, is Jesus Christ (who is also the vine of the vineyard). The vineyard, which experiences the state of dormancy and also relies on the attention of the Gardener during pruning, is the Christian life. Having said that, we must remember that, as Christians, we too may experience a Winter season, and it is during this season that we experience two very unique, yet very necessary processes: dormancy and pruning. Each is a perfect process governed by God's loving and attentive care, where Jesus slowly and gently leads us into the next season, where we are to experience its benefit.

Spiritual Conclusion 1

The first spiritual conclusion of Winter is found in dormancy. For the Christian, this is a time characterized by silence and stagnation. A time where God's voice has become silent and His ear *seems* to have stopped listening to our prayers. A time when our growth in the knowledge of God seems to have come to a sudden halt. It is a trying time during which, like King David, we find ourselves desperately crying out to the God we once conversed with so clearly: "... why are you so far from helping me, and from the words of my groaning? My God I cry in the daytime, but you do not hear..." (Psalm 22:1-2). But yet, it is a silence as precious as God's voice itself. It is not a forsaking silence but rather a prophetic silence heralding the hopeful message of God's coming intimacy. It is a silence that God entrusts us with: an indication that He thinks we can trust Him faithfully without first receiving an audible answer from Him. As Oswald Chambers writes, "When you cannot hear God, you will find that He has trusted you in the most intimate way possible - with absolute silence, not a silence of despair, but one of pleasure, because He saw that you could withstand an even bigger revelation." And if this silence is received as God's gift to us, a gift opened through waiting obediently, we will have in our spiritual possession a faith that is perfectly confident in knowing that God always hears our prayers.

Waiting On God

The Hebrew word for waiting is yachal and it means to trust, to hope, to expect and to remain in a state of patient anticipation. Waiting is an intentionally thoughtful task that relies on an object to wait on. And, it is our level of knowledge about the object and our level of trust in that knowledge as being true, which makes waiting either hopeful or doubtful. The more knowledge we have about the object and the stronger our trust in that knowledge as being true, the more hopeful our waiting will be. The less knowledge we have about the object and the weaker our trust in that knowledge as being true, the more doubtful our waiting will be. The type of waiting one does will matter, not in regards to the eventual truth that the object will reveal, for the truth will still be true regardless of how one waits for that truth. The type of waiting one does will greatly matter in terms of how one experiences that wait, until the truth is finally revealed. A hopeful waiting will come with many moments of joy and fortitude as you wait. A doubtful waiting will come with many moments of worry and despair as you wait. As Christians, the object of our waiting is Jesus Christ- He is the vine and we are the branches. It is, therefore, a greater knowledge of Him and a greater trust in that knowledge of Him as being true, which will ensure that we are able to wait hopefully during the silent and stagnant Winter season. This, we will find, is not something new to the Christian faith, for the Bible is filled with writings of men and woman who waited on God in this way. It is these writings that we should look to for encouragement if we are to make it through our own Winter dormancy. When evil flourishes all around us and the wicked seem to be mocking our stagnant days, we are to do as King David did and " rest in the Lord, and wait patiently for Him" (Psalm 37:7). When God seems to be hiding His face from us while we are being persecuted and forsaken by the ones we love most; even then the advice given to us is to "wait on the Lord; be of good courage..." (Psalm 27:14). When your love for Jesus seems to be like a sword tearing apart the relationship between even your loved ones, even more should your words echo those of Micah, "I will look to the Lord; I will wait for the God of my salvation" (Micah 7:7). When all chances of breakthrough seem impossible and your mind begins to reach for the empty solutions that the world offers, be bold and say, "My soul, wait silently for God alone, for my expectation is from Him" (Psalm 62:5). When people mock your hope in Jesus and say that you are a fanatic or out of your mind, cry out with the prophet Isaiah, "And I will wait on the Lord...I will hope in Him" (Isaiah 8:17). When your mind becomes burdened by the weight of your worry and you can no longer remember the grace of God, even then cry out as David did, "I wait for the Lord, my soul waits, and in His word I do hope" (Psalm 130:5). When the enemy tries to deceive you into believing waiting is futile, be bold and speak truth into that lie, for indeed "It is good that one should hope and wait quietly for the salvation of the Lord" (Lamentations 3:26). The testimonies of those who waited on God have been recorded and sealed in the Bible for all to see. In the words of the prophet Isaiah, "The Lord is good to those who wait for Him, to the soul who seeks Him"(Lamentations 3: 25). As David so faithfully declared, "I waited patiently for the Lord and He inclined to me, and heard my cry" (Psalm 40:1). And as Isaiah boldly stated, "those who wait on the Lord shall renew their strength; they shall mount up with wings like eagles, they shall run and not grow weary, they shall walk and not faint" (Isaiah 40:31). God is faithful to those who wait for Him and if you do wait on the Lord during this season and you trust in His faithfulness, then be sure that God will answer you in His perfect time. For each minute that we wait in silence, the Lion of Judah is fast approaching, eager to break the silence of our waiting with His mighty roar of faithfulness. But, waiting on God is not always easy and often the silence in which we wait goes on for so long that we begin to doubt our waiting. We start to wonder if the silence will break if we are more faithful. We fall into the trap of reasoning out our own faith. When we do this we make ourselves the object of our waiting. Instead of making Jesus the object of our waiting and putting our trust and hope in Him to break the silence, we make our own feelings the object in which we trust. We turn away from the vine and we start looking toward the leaves again. But the leaves have now fallen, and all we have left is the vine.

Fix Your Gaze

Despite realizing that all we have is the vine, we still fail to keep our gaze securely fixed on it; a gaze that would assure a hopeful waiting. Instead, we keep looking toward the bare branches, hopelessly waiting for a leaf to appear that will give us the false confidence to wait some more. But, the leaf doesn't appear, and we are left with our backs toward the vine, waiting in doubt. We must remember that waiting is dependent on the level of knowledge of the object on which we wait and our level of trust in that knowledge as being true. Therefore, remembering also that Jesus is the vine, it is having a greater knowledge of who Jesus is and a stronger trust in that knowledge as being true, that will keep you "looking unto Jesus" (Hebrews 12:2) , that is looking to the vine. The Hebrew word for "looking", as used in Hebrews 12:2, is aphorao and it comes from the Hebrew apo which means "away from" and horao which means "to see". The word means an exclusive attention, looking away from all distractions in order to have your gaze entirely fixed on one object. And, in the context of Hebrews 12:2, "looking unto Jesus" means to have eyes only for Jesus Christ. In the pages to follow I will explain how we should be constantly looking unto Jesus with an undivided attention and it is my hope that, if you determine it in your heart to look unto Jesus in that way as often as you can, with a gaze that's held by trust, then your waiting will be filled with hope and joy, and that it will end with God breaking the silence.

Look to Jesus on the Cross

We must look toward Jesus on the cross. When our mind gazes toward that rocky hill, where the love and wrath of God collided in a passionate display of wisdom, where the hopeless past greeted the hopeful future, and when an eternal choice entered the world, we will find the solution to any problem caused by our waiting. For, at the pinnacle of that rocky hill, elevated above Calvary, we will find our Saviour, Jesus Christ, hanging from a cross: bleeding, agonizing, suffering and dying a sinner's death, for us. We will find the Son of God, perfect in every way, allowing Himself to be blemished so that we would appear spotless. We will find Jesus Christ, "wounded for our transgressions, bruised for our iniquities; the chastisement for our peace" (Isaiah 53:5). Having always that scene readily available in our mind, we can quickly recall it during any spiritual challenge our waiting provides. If our waiting stirs in us troubling thoughts that God's silence is a foreshadowing of His impending wrath, then we look unto Jesus on the cross and remember that He bore the full wrath of God, for "Christ has redeemed us from the curse of the law having become a curse for us..." (Galatians 3:13). Remembering this will give us hope in our waiting, knowing that despite "having sinned and fallen short of God's glory" (Romans 3:23), God will not punish us in the way we deserve, for Jesus took that punishment for us. If we begin to drown in the silence as we wait and start to doubt if God ever loved us, then we look unto Jesus on the cross and remember that "...scarcely for a righteous man will one die..." but God demonstrates His own love toward us, in that while we were still sinners, Christ died for us (Romans 5:7-8). And once more we remember, even though God is silent and the enemy is shooting fiery arrows of deceit toward us about God's love for us, that "God so loved the world that He gave His only begotten Son, that whoever believes in Him should not perish but have everlasting life" (John 3:16). When we look unto Jesus on the cross, we see God's love for us: an unconditional love that always seeks the very best for us. A love that is perfectly comfortable in silence. A love that needs no feeling, no conversation, no affirmation but only an object to love. And we are that object; God's object of everlasting love. So look unto Jesus on the cross and consider how He loves you and find comfort in your waiting. When our waiting causes us to doubt whether we will be able to fix our gaze on the vine of Jesus much longer, we look unto Jesus hanging on the cross and remember that He said, "This is My blood of the new covenant, which is shed for many (Mark 14:24). This new covenant is God's will and contract; He set the terms, decided its conditions and established its purposes. And, Jesus' blood which was shed makes this contract unbreakable and everlasting. It's in the terms of this contract, of which the prophet Jeremiah describes a few, where we will find the promise of God to secure our faith toward Him. God's covenant, made eternal through the blood of Jesus, will ensure that we remain faithful. God's covenant will ensure that inside your heart there is always a fear of Him, for He said, " I will make an everlasting covenant with them...I will put My fear into their hearts so that they will not depart from Me" (Jeremiah 32:40). God's covenant will ensure that as you wait, no matter how long the silence is and how slow the growth is, you will always attempt to look to the vine that is Jesus Christ. We need not fret and attempt to justify our level of faith as we wait. Instead, we should wait with eyes always looking unto Jesus on the cross: grateful for the blood that He shed which secured for us a faith that will always be fixed on Him, our everlasting vine. We must remember that there is nothing that we can do on our own which will give us the peace of God's faithfulness as we wait: no reading the Bible, no serving in Church, no lifting our arms in worship, no acts of goodwill, no praying for hours, no tithing and no fasting. As much as these acts may comfort us for a moment as we wait, they are all worthless and dead works in the matter of our justification and God's faithfulness. The only way that we can feel peace and rest in God's faithfulness while we wait, is to look unto Jesus on the cross and believe that it is only because of Him crucified that we have peace with God. It is only because of Jesus crucified that we are always the objects of God's love and God's faithfulness. So, when we are troubled by God's silence, and we begin to consider that He may not have led us into the peril of Winter for a good cause, then we must look unto Jesus on the cross, for there our eyes will look upon the same scene that the apostle Paul was looking to when he wrote, "He who did not spare His own Son, but delivered Him up for us all, how shall He not with Him also freely give us all things?" (Romans 8:32). This promise to give us "all things" does not refer to giving us everything we need to feel comfortable during this time of waiting but rather it is the promise of giving us all things in order "to be conformed to the image of His Son" (Romans 8:29). It is the promise of giving us all things (like the silence and stagnation of Winter) so that we can, through the process of receiving that thing as a gift from God, be transformed more into the perfected image of Jesus Christ. Therefore, when your mind begins to doubt the end result of this waiting, look unto Jesus on the cross and remember that He suffered and died on the cross so that God would give us all that we need to become more like Jesus. And, as you wait and look unto Jesus, remember also that "...all things work together for good to those who love God..." (Romans 8:28).

Look to Jesus' Return

We must also look forward to Jesus' return as King. To look unto Jesus in this way is to look towards the heavens and see the eternal Son of God return in the clouds with great power and glory (Mark 13:26). To look unto Jesus in this way is to listen for the sound of the seventh Angel's trumpet and hear the voices in heaven declare, "The Kingdoms of this world have become the kingdoms of our Lord and His Christ, and He shall reign forever and ever" (Revelation 11:15). It is to look hopefully toward the day when we see heaven opened and the absolute perfection of Jesus Christ, His eyes radiant like a flame of fire, riding valiantly on a white horse, leading the armies of heaven to claim the eternal victory (Revelation 19:11-14). It is to look toward Jesus, the King of Kings and the Lord of Lords, the Alpha and the Omega, the beginning and the end, and the One who was, and the One who is to come (Revelation 1:8;11:16). For it is to look to Jesus in this way, "for the blessed hope and glorious reappearing of our great God and Saviour Jesus Christ" (Titus 2:13), that we will find the perfect remedy for any doubt and despair that we may experience during our silent Winter season. Although we may become deflated by the perplexity of our waiting, and our joy may be cast down by the weight of the silence, we are to look unto Jesus and remember that He is preparing for us a room in His Father's house. He has not, at all, forgotten about us and when the time is right, He will most certainly come back for us (John 14:2-3). It is only by looking unto Jesus as the coming King that we can sustainabily wait in hope, for it is the only truth that we have regarding the final outcome of our waiting. God can, and by His grace, He will most likely end your waiting well before the second coming of His son, but to truly wait hopefully is to wait with a confidence that regardless of what you experience currently, and regardless of how long you may have to endure it, the final end is certain, and Jesus will restore you and everything around you to its former, purified state. Therefore, whatever it is that you may be waiting on, and whatever God may be silent about, do not let the uncertainties of the future unsettle your mind and rattle the foundation on which you have built your relationship with Jesus. The enemy longs to get you to believe that you will stay as you are and that whatever you are feeling is your own fault and that you will not change or improve or come out of whatever dark cloud you may have found yourself in. But, let me assure you that those are lies; deceitful schemes to get you looking to yourself again as the object of your waiting. The truth is that your restoration, your improvement and your change is certain and already established in Jesus Christ. So, let Him remain the object of your waiting and look unto Him at all times and look forward to the magnificent event of His second coming. Let your mind daily look unto this scene and let that calm your mind and create hope in your soul while you wait. You need not despair, not even in the most silent, stagnant or gloomiest hour, for your waiting is but a vapour that will one day evaporate into the everlasting joy of God's presence.

Spiritual Conclusion 2

The second spiritual conclusion of Winter is found in the pruning of the branches. For the Christian, pruning is a time when our Gardener, Jesus, removes two inhibitors to the growth of our spiritual fruit. The first is the removal of the unproductive works of our flesh and the second is the removal of any distractions which deviate us from our source of support, and our true vine, Jesus . The unproductive works of the flesh include: adultery, fornication, sexual immorality, idolatry, sorcery, hatred, contentions, jealousies, outbursts of wrath, selfish ambitions, dissensions and heresies (Galatians 5:19-22). The distractions, which are very often the incubators of these works of the flesh, can include a wide variety of things which are very much dependent on one's circumstances. To name just a few for the sake of having an example, they include: certain friendships, access to finances, career paths and even success. Pruning, just like dormancy, can be a terribly difficult time for a new Christian experiencing it for the first time. However, it is also definitely a process that does not end in defeat, but instead can be overcome through perseverance. According to the Oxford Dictionary, perseverance means to "continue in a course of action in spite of difficulty or with little or no indications of success." For a Christian, to persevere means to remain on the path of faithfulness in the face of trying circumstances. It means to remain faithful to Jesus Christ even when you cannot see a way out of the difficult situation you find yourself in.

It means to deny yourself, and take up your cross daily, and follow Jesus (Luke 9:23). Persevering as a Christian means to reject the pleasures of a comfortable life and to continue the pursuit of holiness even if it means suffering during that pursuit.

Look to Jesus at the Right Hand of God

In order to persevere, we must look to Jesus seated at the right hand of God. When we look to Jesus in this way we will find Jesus Christ, the Man who was blindfolded and beaten, mocked and spat on, now alive and strong, sitting at the right hand of the power of God (Luke 22:69). We will see Jesus, the man who once walked like a lonely lamb to the slaughter, carrying the weight of a wooden cross on His bleeding back, now sitting beside His Father in heaven "crowned with glory and honour..." (Hebrews 2:9) and "worthy... to receive power and riches and wisdom" (Revelation 5:12). When we look unto Jesus in this way we will see a Great King in heaven who "for the joy that was set before Him, endured the cross, despising the shame, and is seated at the right hand of the throne of God" (Hebrews 12:2). It is only by looking unto Jesus in this way that we find the source of true perseverance to endure our suffering. When Jesus was exalted to the right hand of God, He became more than just the atonement for our sins; He became our High Priest and Representative. And there in heaven, as our High Priest, He lives to intercede for us; always pleading our cause before the Father. He is always willing to obtain for us mercy and grace. He is always sympathizing with our suffering; listening to our confessions. He is always willing to strengthen us when we are weak, to comfort us when we are afflicted, to remind us not to worry and to guide us in righteousness, giving us all that we need to persevere along the difficult path of faithfulness. (Hebrews 4:14-16, Romans 8:34, Philippians 4:13, 2 Corinthians 1:3, Mathew 6:25, Psalm 23:3). When we look unto Jesus sitting at the right hand of God, we see a mighty and loyal friend who promises to never leave us, to never forget us and to never abandon us (Hebrews 11:14). By looking unto Jesus in this way, we see not only the light of hope shining on all kinds of suffering, but we see the way, which is through Jesus Christ our High Priest, to access the power that enabled Him to persevere during His great suffering, and that is the power of grace from God in heaven.

We are also to look unto Jesus as our Gardener, the one who was very much a man. When we look unto Jesus in this way, we will see a human being who was very much like you and me. He was born of a woman (Luke 2:7), He was flesh and blood (Philippians 2:5-8), He grew up over the years into an adult (Luke 2:52), He got hungry and ate (Mark 11:12), He got thirsty and drank (John 19:28), He walked and got tired (John 4:6), He rested and slept (Matthew 8:24), He wept and even got angry (John 11:35,38). When we look to Jesus in this way, we will see a man who, although fully God and the Eternal King, at a certain point in history entered the world as an incarnation of God in human form. He was fully God and fully human. J.C. Ryle writes, "I see a marvelous proof of love and wisdom in the union of two natures in Christ's person...almighty power and deepest sympathy are met together in one glorious person, Jesus Christ, my Lord." It is by looking unto Jesus in this way, that we begin to understand the powerful truth that our mighty God and High Priest, who has everything in this world under His authority (Ephesians 1:22), is able to sympathize with our feelings and emotions and experiences on the most relatable level possible. As a man, He experienced every emotional experience that this life has to offer, with the exception of sin. He experienced the heartbreaking numbness of loss (Matthew 14:13), the unbearable pain of abuse (John 19:1), the frightening reality of not having a home (Luke 9:58), the bitter hurt of being persecuted (John 19:2-4), the mental anguish of being tempted (Matthew 4:1), the sad disappointment of being betrayed (Matthew 26:21) and the dark loneliness of being forsaken (Matthew 27:46). In the final three years that Jesus lived on earth, He drank mostly from the cup of hardship and sorrow. Jesus, our Gardener, the one who walks in the vineyard and gently holds the branch in His hands, as He intentionally and delicately prunes away the unproductive parts of our lives that would otherwise kill us if left to grow, is not unaware of what we are feeling. He not only knows the deepest parts of our hearts and what we are feeling, but He also knows exactly what that feeling feels like. He can relate to us on an experiential level, for He too has felt the anguish that we feel. Jesus Christ knows exactly what we are going through and His heart breaks with ours. But He also loves us dearly and knows exactly what He is doing. Jesus is in control. And, if the knowledge that it is the loving Lord Jesus who is doing the actual pruning in our life is not enough to give us the hope to persevere, then we must look unto Jesus, the one who can truly comfort us in our most painful moments, the one who never grows weary of hearing our cries and the one who will never stop loving us and pleading our cause before our Father in heaven. Jesus experienced it all and persevered to a glorious destination so that we, through Him and by His Spirit, can persevere to the same glorious destination.

Winter is not an easy season to endure. If God has brought you into a Winter season and you are experiencing the confusing silence of dormancy and the discomforting jerks of pruning, do not find it unusual to find yourself begging God to answer your desperate questions of "why me?" and "how long still?" and to come before Him with eyes filled with heavy tears. If your life has been one of seeking Jesus, living righteously and repenting for where you fall short of His holiness, then take heart, for this is a season where God is merely taking you deeper in your faith and bringing you closer to the ripeness of your fruit. A season where the tears you sow in humble confession before the Lord, will reap an abundant harvest of joy with the Lord (Psalm 126:5). It will be a season where God is creating in you an unquestionable faith to trust Him in the matter of your justification, sanctification and perseverance. It is in this time that we must understand, with absolute clarity, that the Christian life is indeed one that will lead us into difficult circumstances and it is necessary for every young Christian to understand that what you may be experiencing in your spiritual life, in particular with regards to feelings of fear, unbelief and doubt, may be as a result of a true faith and grace and not because of a lack in that area, which is what your enemy, the accuser and liar, the devil would have you believe. For the Christian life, the one lived not in public title, but in spiritual practise, is a life that is not secure from trials and sufferings nor will it ever be. The truly Christian life is lived with an understanding that, along the path of faithfulness, we are often met with unexpected obstacles of loss and sorrow, hardship and disappointment, temptations and pain and trials and tribulations. It is a life that understands and accepts that Jesus never promised us a life free from the perils of the world, but rather promised us that if we remain on the path of faithfulness then "...in all these things we are more than conquerors through Him who loved us" (Romans 8:37). And this is a love that has never abandoned any saint that has lived his life walking along this path that we too find ourselves on. It is a love that will never abandon any true saint of Jesus that remains on its narrow course. And I, like the determined Saint Paul, "am persuaded that neither death nor life, nor angels nor principalities, nor powers, nor things present, nor things to come, nor height nor depth, nor any other created thing, shall be able to separate us from the love of God which is in

Christ Jesus our Lord" (Romans 8:38-39). And, it is by keeping our gaze toward this love in Christ, that we will continue to be sanctified by God and preserved by Jesus Christ, as we walk along the path of faithfulness (Jude 1:1).

Practical Applications

Before we end this chapter I would like to conclude with three points of practical application that may be useful if you find yourself in a Winter season.

Guard Against False Comforts

Firstly, in this time you may very likely be drawn to many false comforts which can provide you with a sense of security, a peacefulness, or an unrealistic assurance that what you may be doubting or what trial you may be experiencing, is not God's will for your life. What could draw you to them is your own deceitful heart (still being in the flesh and not yet fully perfected in Christ, our heart is still prone to wickedness) which craves an immediate feeling of peace and assurance. You could also be drawn to them by the temptations of the enemy who offers you this false comfort as a way to distract you from looking unto Jesus in this difficult time. Very often it is a combination of our deceitful heart and the temptations of the enemy which lead us off the path of faithfulness toward the false comforts. However appealing and accessible these comforts may seem, they can only offer, if anything at all, a temporary solution for your struggle. In the end you will find yourself in a far worse position than you were before you pursued them. These false comforts may be found in the content-rich material of certain pastors' sermons, certain worship songs, certain Christian books and on certain Christian blogs and websites. These are presented on a Christian platter by individuals or institutions that claim to be true Christians. Now, many of them may indeed be true Christians and the false comfort which they offer may, by no means be an intentional desire to preach a false doctrine, but rather be the result of a shallow understanding of that doctrine and a poor manner of stating that doctrine, so they end up preaching false comforts which are not true to the actual word of God. However, many of these proclaiming Christians may indeed be false preachers who are intentionally preaching false doctrine and false comforts to distract you from looking unto Jesus. The Bible warns us of them, telling us to "beware of false prophets, who come to you in sheep's clothing, but inwardly they are ravenous wolves" (Matthew 7:15). Considering this difficulty of having to discern between truth and falsehood, our first instinct may then be to stay away from all Christian material entirely and rather spend time alone with God reading only the Bible and praying only by ourselves. However, this would be a mistake. We should attend Church and equip ourselves with Christian material because the Bible clearly states the following: "Let the word of Christ dwell in you richly in all wisdom, teaching and admonishing one another in psalms and hymns and spiritual songs, singing with grace in your hearts to the Lord" (Colossians 3:16) and that we should "consider one another in order to stir up love and good works, not forsaking the assembly of ourselves together...but exhorting one another..." (Hebrews 10:24-25). It is in this regard that we are to be "...wise as serpents and harmless as doves" (Matthew 10:16). We need to be wise in identifying which word is of Christ and therefore true, and which word is of the world and therefore false. To do this, we need to make sure that every piece of Christian material that we consume, be it in the form of a sermon, a song, a book, a poem, or a blog post, is tested by what it says in the Bible. The Sixth Article of the Church of England should serve us well in this regard: "Holy Scripture containeth all things necessary to salvation: so that whatsoever is not read therein, nor may be proved thereby, is not required of any man, that it should be believed as an article of the Faith, or be thought requisite or necessary to salvation." And so, when the false comforts come your way, remember this rule and let it be engraved in the deepest part of your mind so that you will always have readily available the reminder not to believe any word of comfort spoken by even the most truthful and Holy Christian alive, unless it can be proved by what is written in the Holy Bible, for as J.C. Ryle writes: "One plain verse of scripture, to my mind, outweighs the most logical conclusions to which human reason can attain."

Know Jesus Deeper

The second practical application that I wish to present to you is the regular and honest pursuit of knowing Jesus Christ. As we have seen throughout this chapter, Winter is a season that requires us to wait and persevere by looking unto Jesus.

Your experience of waiting and persevering will be more hopeful if you have a greater knowledge of who Jesus is. In Matthew, Mark, Luke and John, we have four different eye-witness accounts of who Jesus is and collectively these four books provide us with the most accurate piece of historical literature about the life of Jesus Christ. Therefore, it is without question that these four books are the closest document we have to a biography of Jesus and, therefore, the most comprehensive information available if you desire to know more about who He is and what happened during the three years of His ministry. I therefore encourage you to read the four gospels of the Bible more frequently so that you can acquire a greater knowledge and understanding of who Jesus is. It is by reading these four books, with their unique perspectives and insights, that you will become more familiar with the One who is asking you to wait patiently and persevere during this difficult season. Once you truly know the character and nature of the One who is asking you to wait and persevere, you will be able to do it with hope and expectation that the outcome will be glorious.

Have Compassion

The third and final practical application that I wish to leave with you is that of having a compassionate heart towards those Christian brothers and sisters who find themselves in a Winter season. There are many Christians who are greatly troubled by fear and anxiety over their spiritual condition. There are many Christians who, although honest believers of Christ and who truly long to serve Him, find themselves overcome with doubt about their justification, the grace they have received, the unending love that Christ has for them and the hope that is in Christ. Many Christians who are experiencing the silence of Winter and being asked to wait and persevere with Jesus Christ, are losing their hope and slowly beginning to fade away from their first love. They are like the father of the sick child in the book of Mark, crying to God and saying, "...Lord, I believe, help me in my unbelief" (Mark 9:24). Like David they say, " now I shall perish someday...there is nothing better for me...I shall escape out of this land" (1 Samuel 27:1). And like Job they despairingly ask, "Where then is my hope...who can see it?" (Job 17:15). I ask the Church then to be cautious in assuming that those Christians who have their hope in Jesus and who know that their salvation is in Jesus Christ, have turned away intentionally from God. Be wary of saying to yourself, "if only they kept their eyes fixed on Jesus...." For it may well be a case of them having done exactly that which has led them into this season of doubt. The faithful and loyal apostles of Jesus became doubtful and fearful the very moment they went through a storm. Not one of us has yet been perfected in Christ and until our bodies are raised from the dead, we are still susceptible to the occasional struggles of doubt and fear. Sympathize with these Christians and do not cast them off. Pray with them and be the comforting arms of Jesus Christ. Fast with them and believe together for their breakthrough. Be great intercessors on their behalf and earnestly pray that God would ignite the fire in their soul again and restore to them the joy, peace, love and confidence of their Saviour, Jesus Christ. The command Jesus spoke in John 13:34 : "...that you love one another; as I have loved you..." is more necessary than ever before. Let us not forget the kind of love expected from us by Jesus Christ, and may we never forget Jesus Christ in the pursuit of loving others.

Winter has been long and difficult, but God has been by our side the entire time and has preserved us through the coldest and darkest days. And now, suddenly, the dawn seems to be breaking sooner and the last daylight seems to be leaving later. A swallow has appeared overhead, and comes to rest on the fragile branches. In the blink of an eye, the whole vineyard is a symphony of chirping birds, sharing the many stories of their Winter travels. The pale sky seems to have taken colour from the sun and spreads its bright blue arms, as if stretching after a deep sleep, pushing the clouds further away with every reach. By the grace of God, Winter is over and Spring has arrived.

DIVINE PURPOSE

Chapter 3

Spring

❝My beloved spoke and said to me: Rise up my love, my fair one, and come away. For lo, the Winter is past, the rain is over and gone. The flowers appear on the earth; the time of singing has come..." (Song of Solomon 2: 11-12). The Lord has spoken; breaking the frozen silence of our cold and lonely Winter. From the once silent corners of the vineyard, we begin to hear the sounds of His praise being lifted up. From everywhere in the vineyard, under the spotlight of the warmer sun and in front of a Spring canvas of seaside blue, soft white, buttercup yellow and apple green, God's creatures begin to lead His vineyard in a concert of thankful praise. Spring time has finally arrived; a time for all creation to rejoice and remember the faithfulness of God. With Spring comes the chance for us to tune our hearts to the melody of heaven again and offer our voice in songs of humble thanksgiving. God has remained faithful; not forsaking us in the silence of winter, but rather leading us out of Winter into the newness of Spring. Spring is a time during which our faith will be stronger and our joy will be deeper. It is a time, if we continue in faithful obedience, in which we will see the first fruits of our waiting begin to blossom from the branches of the vine. It is a blossoming that will gradually take place following three natural processes: bud-break, flowering and fruit-set. Again, it should be noted that each of these natural processes are governed by complex physiological systems which have been carefully studied. However, since we only need a foundational context deep enough to deduce further spiritual conclusions, I will side-step the deep physiological complexities of each process and rather provide a layman overview which will suffice in achieving our objective.

Bud-break

The first natural principle is bud-break. Each bud is an undeveloped embryonic shoot which contains all the material that will eventually form all the components of the living plant: leaves, flowers and fruit. During dormancy, which took place in Winter, these buds were prevented from growing and, therefore, remained closed. But now, with the increase in temperature that Spring brings, the soil begins to warm up, awakening the sleeping vineyard. The Xylem and Phloem (the "arteries" in the plant which transport water and nutrients respectively) unblock, and begin to absorb water and nutrients from the soil and transport them to the tiny buds. The buds begin to fill with a new supply of water and nutrients until eventually, in a glorious display of newness, the buds break open and reveal the new leaf shoots. Most of these new leaf shoots will continue to grow into large green leaves, with a select few, more complex, leaf shoots eventually developing into the flowers that will one day form the fruit. Bud-break is a refreshing and joyful time in the vineyard because it announces the end of the long Winter dormancy and anticipates the arrival of an abundant crop. There are, however, two important considerations to note during bud-break. The first is the timing of bud-break. If the buds break too early, that is closer to the end of Winter as opposed to the start of Spring, then the young leaf shoot that forms would most likely not be capable of surviving the last little bit of Winter. However, the timing of bud-break, if the vineyard is not subjected to unnatural human interventions to speed up dormancy, is always perfect in establishing the desired outcome that God intends for it. Successful bud-break depends on the natural timing of dormancy and bud-break. Any human intervention to speed up the process of dormancy may result in the first leaf shoots being immature, fragile and prone to damage. The second consideration is the impact that grape variety (variety is established by the difference in characteristics of the various grapes that will form) has on the timing of bud-break. Depending on the elevation of the vineyard and also the micro-climate that the vineyard lives in, bud-break can occur earlier for certain varietals while others will experience a longer dormancy.

Flowering

The second natural principle in Spring is flowering. This is the very delicate time in the vineyard when, about two months since the initial bud-break, the more complex leaf shoots begin to develop into flowers. The flowering process begins with the development of tiny green spheres called "calyptras". These little green balls serve as protective lids on top of the developing flower, providing further protection in addition to the large leaves. Although these calyptras resemble miniature green grapes, they are, in fact, only a protective package for the grapes that will form. The flowers develop within the safety of the calyptras lids until the lids burst open and reveal the basic reproductive structures of the perfect flower: the pistil and a stamen. Many such flowers will develop along the length of the branch and form clusters called inflorescence. Flowering is a special time in the vineyard, as the very structures that will one day produce the fruit of the vineyard are starting to develop, comfortably tucked away beneath the big green leaves and safe from any external threats. There are two important considerations to keep in mind as flowering takes place in the vineyard. The first is the threat of pests and insects that are drawn to the vineyard during this time. The clusters of new flowers begin to emit subtle, beautiful fragrances of floral and honey that fill the vineyard with sweet and pleasing aromas. It is these aromas which unintentionally attract dangerous pests and insects to the vineyard; pests and insects that may not have any intention of destroying the new flower but will nonetheless do so in their pursuit of finding and eating the source of the sweet aroma. The second consideration is the effect that a lack of water has on the health of the flowers. A lack of water damages the flowers and results in a smaller crop and grapes of a poor quality.

Fruit-set

The third and final natural principle that we find in Spring is fruit-set. This is when the flower clusters develop into little berries. The flowers that form during flowering are referred to as "perfect flowers", as they contain both of the reproductive structures needed for producing fruit: the pistil and the stamen. During fruit-set, the stamen gently transfers deposits of pollen onto the pistil, until they are all pollinated. Once the pistils are pollinated, the flowers develop into small, hard green berries, each one about the size of a pea. It is these berries that will grow and develop on the branches, well into Summer, until they become the matured, sweet and pleasing grapes that the vineyard owner and the gardener intended to grow. There is one consideration of fruit-set that we should take note of, and that is the uniqueness of self pollination. Since the flowers produced are "perfect-flowers" that contain both the pistil and the stamen, they make use of self-pollination which takes place without the assistance of any external carriers, such as bees or wind, that would otherwise have had to transport pollen between neighbouring stamen and pistil. This unique trait of being self-pollinating is important for two reasons. Firstly, it ensures that the berries which are formed are always pure and never develop from a different and possibly impure pollen; a risk that is possible if external carriers bring foreign pollen strains. Secondly, it ensures that the flowers do not need to do any additional work to attract external carriers, such as developing colourful structures on their surface.

Having equipped ourselves with the knowledge of the natural principles that govern the vineyard during Spring, we are able to deduce the spiritual conclusions relevant to each natural principle. And just as we have aimed to do in both Autumn and Winter, we will discover that by looking deeper, and with faith, into the natural world which God has created, and by being led by God's wisdom and the truth of His word, we are able to deduce wonderful conclusions of spiritual relevance to the Christian life; which if understood and applied, will contribute toward us living a more fruitful life.

Spiritual Conclusion 1

The first spiritual conclusion that we can deduce from Spring is found in bud-break. For a Christian, bud-break refers to the breaking through of our spiritual comfort. If we remember from the first chapter, spiritual comforts are "the feelings we experience as a result of being in God's presence". It was these spiritual comforts that God removed during our spiritual Autumn so that we would be transformed from having an experiential "false-faith" built on those comforts, to having a steadfast "true-faith" built on the person of Jesus Christ. And, having indeed built that type of faith during Winter, it is my belief and conviction that God restores to us our spiritual comforts in Spring, so that we can, once again, experience the comfort of His presence, but this time without the possibility of us detrimentally misplacing our faith in those comforts.

Spiritual Comforts and Spiritual Fruit

Before we continue, it is important for us to distinguish between spiritual comforts and spiritual fruit. Whereas spiritual comforts are the temporary experiences we have as a result of being in God's presence, spiritual fruit is the characteristics of God that can be identified in our lives as a result of God's presence being manifested in us and which can be identified by others. It is important to clearly distinguish the difference between spiritual comfort and spiritual fruit, so that you do not incorrectly assume that the feelings of comfort that take place during bud-break are indications that the fruit of the spirit are already manifested in your life. Although, during bud-break, you may once again experience feelings of joy, peace, kindness, self-control, love, gentleness, patience, goodness and faithfulness, it is my belief that our spiritual comforts must develop into our established spiritual fruit. For as we behold the glory of God while in His presence, we are continually transformed into the same image (2 Corinthians 3:18). The more we come into the presence of God and experience the comfort of His glory, the more we will display His glory. Although these feelings of comfort may not yet be the spiritual fruit we long to have displayed in our life, they are great signs of God's faithfulness and therefore reason enough to rejoice and give God thanks (Zechariah 4:10). If we do not lose heart and do not grow weary, then in due season we will reap the fruit of our faith (Galatians 6:9) and our lives will begin to display the manifest glory of God as He intended.

In the natural, there are two considerations which we have discussed as being pertinent to bud-break: timing and variety. And in each, there are valuable spiritual considerations for us to note.

43

Timing

There may very well come a moment during your spiritual Spring when you question God's timing. You may begin to look around and see how good your life is now and wonder how much better it might have been if God had acted a lot sooner. If that is indeed something you are doing, or if it is perhaps something you might end up doing, let me encourage you to put away such thinking as soon as you can, for it will result in you seeing the blessings present in your life today as faded and delayed. Remember, God's timing for your bud-break is perfect. We know that His timing is perfect because in Hebrews we are told to "...come boldly to the throne of grace, that we may obtain mercy and find grace to help in time of need" (Hebrews 4:16). The interpretation of this verse is that God will provide the help we need at the time when we need it most. Knowing that God's ways are higher than our ways (Isaiah 55:9), we can rest knowing that He knows exactly when our need is indeed most desperate and that He promises to provide a help which is perfectly timed. Although it is indeed perfectly timed, it is not always perfectly on time according to us, "for a thousand years in Your sight are like yesterday when it is past..." (Psalm 90:4). Therefore, let us not be discouraged by the timing of our bud-break but instead let us trust the timing of God and reflect on the example that David set in Psalm 31:15 when he said, "But as for me, I trust in you, O Lord; I say 'You are my God.' My times are in Your hand." We must not consider what might have been, for Jesus has told us that the one who looks back is not fit for the Kingdom of heaven (Luke 9:62).

Variety

Variety, as we have seen, influences the duration of dormancy and consequent onset of bud-break. Spiritually, this variety is present in the vineyard due to the uniqueness of our spiritual being which God created. Every aspect of our being has been carefully woven together by the perfect craftsmanship of God's creative hands to form a being that is wonderful and good in God's sight (Psalm 139:13-14; Genesis 1:31). God has given each one of us unique creational gifts that further enhance our uniqueness (Romans 12:6). Therefore, as uniquely created beings, we can say with a clear understanding that, "by the grace of God I am what I am..." (1 Corinthians 15:10). You and I are precisely what you and I are. There is an absolute uniqueness and divine distinction between each one of us in God's sight. Who I am is exactly who God created me to be and who you are is exactly who God created you to be. Therefore, being so unique and distinct in God's sight, it should not seem at all unreasonable that when God says, "For I know the thoughts that I think toward you..." (Jeremiah 29:11), that He means He has a unique plan for our life that is absolutely distinct from anyone else's. So, it should not at all surprise us that some of us may experience a shorter or longer dormancy period than others and, as a result, the timing of our bud-break may very well differ from that of many other Christians that are around us.

It is essential that we come to terms with the divine uniqueness of our created being and the particular timing of our spiritual development. If we are tempted to compare the timing of our bud-break to that of others, we must tell ourselves that to compare the timing of our bud-break to that of others is an illogical and irrational act, for God has created us with absolute distinction from others and has a particular plan for our lives. If we fail to remember that the timing of our bud-break was perfectly planned according to God's will for our life we will begin to replace the truth, that God's glory is present in our unique timing, with the lies that our own imperfections caused our bud to break at an unfavorable time.

Spiritual Conclusion 2

The second spiritual conclusion that we can deduce from Spring is found in flowering. For a Christian, flowering is the time when, as a result of obediently coming into God's presence and beholding His glory, our lives noticeably start to transform into that same glory (2 Corinthians 3:18). It is a time when our spiritual comforts begin to transform from mere experiences of God's glory to actual displays of His glory. God begins to manifest His presence in our lives and, as a result, our lives begin to release the sweet fragrance of Christ. During this time we become aware of the fact, or are made aware of it by others, that we do some things differently to the way we used to do them. We will also begin to see how this new, and very much improved, way of living brings a better outcome for ourselves and for those around us. We become aware of moments when we have a much deeper joy than what we once knew and find ourselves in a state of rest or calmness without striving to feel calm. We begin to notice the ease with which we are able to pardon the faults of others while remaining even-tempered and tranquil as we see their faults surfacing. We notice how unaffected we are by the persecutions and slander of our enemies, enduring all the hurtful things they say without feeling an urge to take revenge. We start to notice a greater certainty of how we perceive God's love for us; a certainty which creates in us a steady understanding of who Jesus is. We start to notice the ease with which we are able to ignore negative temptations. We become gripped by a powerful desire to do the right thing in every situation in which we find ourselves. We develop a compassion towards others which urges us to provide help and care. Finally, we begin to love others in such a way that our concern is no longer for ourselves but solely for others. In whatever area it is in our life that we begin to notice significant changes for the better, if we have indeed been obediently spending more time with God in His word, then these new behaviours are the direct result of what Paul refers to in 2 Corinthians 2:14 when he says, "Now thanks be to God, who always leads us in triumph in Christ, and through us diffuses the fragrance of His knowledge in every place." Our lives have started to emit the fragrance of Christ; an aroma capable of pleasing the sense of anyone who experiences it, and which lingers in one's thoughts long after it first arrived. Our old, destructive and rotting sinful scent which we used to emit has given way to the beautiful aroma of the life of Jesus, for it is no longer our old, sinful nature that lives, but rather Christ that lives in us (Galatians 2:20).

As we have seen by looking at the natural principles of Spring, the spiritual flowering which a Christian experiences is an extremely delicate time. It is this delicacy which makes it so important to fully understand the two considerations relevant to a Christian during this time.

Spiritual Attack

The first consideration is that of spiritual attack. When we begin to live lives in humble obedience to God, and as a result He begins to manifest the character of Jesus in our lives which gives off the beautiful aroma of His fragrance, then we begin to attract the enemy. The enemy is not drawn by a pleasurable desire for the aroma. The enemy is drawn to the aroma out of a bitter hate for the aroma and, therefore, has a determined will to suppress the release of that aroma. As Christians who submit to God and through whom God displays His glory, we have to understand the reality that we have a supernatural enemy whose aim is to hurt us, deceive us, distract us and to destroy anything in our lives that displays God's glory. The Bible calls Him the devil and Satan (Revelation 12:9) and he "...walks about like a roaring lion, seeking whom he may devour" (1 Peter 5:8). In Chapter six we will discuss "Spiritual Warfare" in depth, but for now it is only necessary to be aware that during this time of spiritual flowering, when the fruit of the spirit is starting to blossom in our lives and God is displaying more of the glory of Jesus through our lives, the enemy will attempt to prevent any further spiritual growth from taking place. However, this knowledge of a possible attack must not be received with any fear of how the enemy will attack us or with doubts about whether we will survive the attack. Jesus' blood, shed on Calvary, claimed the victory over the devil (Revelation 12:11) on our behalf. So then, although at times the battle may not be easy, the outcome of victory is certain (Revelation 20:10). Therefore, we need not fear. Rather, we are to stand firm in our faith (1 Peter 5:9) remembering at all times that our lives are secure in Jesus and that we share in His victory over the devil. And, as good soldiers of Jesus Christ (2 Timothy 2:3), we are to rejoice in any battles we have to endure, for they are indications that God is using our lives for His glory. Our duty then is simple: pray without ceasing (1 Thessalonians 5:16-17) and continue to wage warfare against our enemy (1 Timothy 1:18).

Spiritual Nourishment

The second consideration which we need to remember during this time is the necessity to remain spiritually nourished. As we have seen in the natural, the inflorescence (the cluster of new flowers) requires a consistent and substantial supply of water if the flowers are to maintain a healthy growth. It is this healthy flower growth which will ensure a fruit yield that is of good quality and sufficient quantity. If our lives are to yield any spiritual fruit that is of a high quality and quantity, we need to ensure that we are spiritually nourished daily. The only source of this spiritual nourishment is provided by the word of God. We know this because in Deuteronomy 8:3 Moses tells us, "...man shall not live by bread alone; but man lives by every word that proceeds from the mouth of the Lord." And so it is the same by reading the Holy scriptures found in the Bible, because they are the actual living words of God. 2 Timothy 3:16 says, "All scripture is given by inspiration of God..." The Greek word theopneustos, translated "inspiration of God", literally means "God-breathed". Therefore this verse can be rephrased by saying, " All scripture, that is to say everything written in the Holy Bible, contains in it the breath of God." We have in our possession the Holy Bible as the absolute source of all spiritual nourishment and it's not because its content was written by individuals with enlightened human reason and logic that it is the only source of spiritual nourishment, but rather because it has within each word, even to the small letter "i" (Luke 16:17), the actual living breath of God which gives life to everything. Each word consumed, therefore, nourishes us spiritually in the same way each breath of air consumed, nourishes us physically. As Christians experiencing the development of spiritual fruit, we require the spiritual nourishment of God's word as desperately as a newborn baby requires milk (1 Peter 2:2). Therefore, we should be diligent in spending time in the word of God, "rightly dividing the word of truth" (2 Timothy 2:15). We should be energetic, active, and earnest in studying the word of God, desiring only the razorsharp, most truthful, straight-on application of the word. Without this kind of pursuit for the word of God, our spiritual flowers will become spiritually parched, eventually wilting from a thirst which could only have been satisfied by the word of God. However, as spiritually necessary as this desire for God's word is, the time spent in God's word should not be undertaken as a legal duty, but rather as a humble responsibility to remain obedient to God. Although we are not bound by legal obligation to read the word of God, we must still understand that the degree to which we are able to love Jesus is very much the degree to which we seek and obey the word of God. In John 14:21 Jesus says, "He who has My commandments and keeps them, it is he who loves Me." For it is these commandments found in the word of God, which are the pathway to knowing Jesus well (John 5:39) and it is by knowing Jesus well, that we are able to love Jesus honestly. It is by loving Jesus honestly, that we become vessels of honour for His glory (2 Timothy 2:21). Therefore, let us feed from the word of God every day, for "it shall never return void, and from it shall always come a fruitful harvest" (Isaiah 55:10-11).

Spiritual Conclusion 3

The third, and final spiritual conclusion that Spring provides us, is fruit-set. This is the time in the life of a Christian when it becomes clear that God has established several characteristics of Jesus in our lives. It is the time when the fruit of God, although not yet fully developed, is clearly identifiable in our lives. It is a time where others can look to us and say with an honest conviction that we do indeed have as characteristics of our lives, the joy, peace, kindness, self-control, love, gentleness, patience, goodness and faithfulness of Jesus (Galatians 5:22-23). It may, however, not necessarily be all of them displayed in full glory at once. It may be only one of them for now, displayed in a true and consistent way. Whichever fruit may have set and is now starting to ripen, we must always remember that the end to which we long to have this fruit fully ripe in our lives, should not be for our own pleasure and satisfaction, but rather for the glorification of God. In John 15:8 Jesus tells us, " By this my Father is glorified, that you bear much fruit; so you will be my disciples." The purpose of our lives yielding fruit is not, ultimately, so that we get to enjoy for ourselves the joy, peace, kindness, self-control, love, gentleness, patience, goodness and faithfulness that it will no doubt give us, but rather it is so that we will, being enabled by those very characteristics, live lives that will make us worthy of being called disciples of Jesus. Therefore, the purpose of our yielding fruit is so that we will be enabled to full-heartedly follow the ways of Jesus and worship Him exclusively in spirit and truth (John 4:23-24). It is so that we will be able to humble ourselves in willing service to others (Mark 10:45). It is so that we will love others the way Jesus loved us (John 15:12). And, it is so that we will go out into the world and tell everybody about the wonderfully good news that, "...God so loved the world that He gave His only begotten Son, that whoever believes in Him should not perish but have everlasting life" (Mark 16:15; John 3:16). In essence, it is the fruit of our lives which enables the discipleship and it is the discipleship which glorifies God.

In the natural vineyard, we discussed the important consideration of self-pollination, a process which characterizes "perfect flowers", and which I mentioned as being unique to the vineyard with regards to how the fruit-set took place. It is that principle of self-pollination that we will now use to infer a paralleled spiritual consideration equally as important to our spiritual fruit-set. In the same way that the vineyard flower produces fruit entirely from within itself by self-pollination and does not need to do anything to attract any external carrier to help produce fruit, so the fruit that develops and ripens in our lives is the result of the Holy Spirit working within us. We do not need to do any works to produce the fruit of our lives. In order for this to make sense, we must remember that our justification by faith is already settled. We are in right standing with God because we have put our faith in Jesus Christ as our Saviour, wisdom and righteousness (Philippians 3:9; 1 Corinthians 1:30). We cannot become more righteous through doing good works. Our fruit cannot be the result of righteousness, for then we would have had fruit the moment we were justified and made righteous. Although the fruit is indeed of righteousness, in that it is conformed to the will of God, it is not attained through righteousness, but rather it is attained by Jesus Christ (Philippians 1:11). How it is attained by Jesus Christ is explained to us in the book of John. In John 15:4 Jesus tells us, "...the branch cannot bear fruit of itself, unless it abides in the vine, neither can you, unless you abide in Me." It is then clear that the only way in which our lives can bear fruit, is if we obediently abide in our true vine, Jesus Christ. For, it is only through Jesus that we receive the power of the Holy Spirit (John 7:39; Acts 2:33), and it is only by the power of the Holy Spirit working within us that we are then transformed, by the renewing of our minds, into the likeness of Jesus Christ (Romans 12:2; 2 Corinthians 3:18). And, it is only by being transformed into the likeness of Jesus Christ that our lives bear fruit. In essence, the fruit which we bear is the likeness of Jesus Christ on display. Therefore, we should put behind us any attempts to bear fruit through legalistic, righteous living, for such striving will prove to be an unproductive burden inhibiting any fruit growth. Instead, we should take upon ourselves the yoke of Jesus Christ and allow Him to gently lead us into a relationship of abiding in Him. For "...His yoke is easy and His burden is light..." (Matthew 11:30) and it is the only way in which we will find rest for our souls (Matthew 11:29) and, simultaneously, bear fruit.

Practical Applications

The spiritual Spring which God has led us into is a season in which we can fully delight in God and in the good work He has done, and is still doing, in our lives. The way to experience that joy is through obedience to what God asks of us in this time. In the pages to follow I will provide three practical applications from God's word which will guide us to enjoy God more fully as we experience Spring and are led into Summer. They are the obedience of resting in Jesus, the obedience of remembering God's faithfulness and the obedience of rejoicing in God. Rest, remember, rejoice; three words that are easy to recall and necessary to understand if you are to honour God's faithfulness and goodness which He has revealed to us in Spring.

Rest

The Greek word for rest is anapauo, and it is translated "to make to cease". The word describes a discontinuation from toil and a rejuvenation. In the context of our practical application, to rest in Jesus means that, by faithfully putting our hope to bear fruit in Jesus alone, we are able to stop looking at our own ability and circumstances to bear the fruit and, as a result, we are rejuvenated or refreshed. To find this rest in Jesus is not difficult. All it requires, is for us to do the very simple action of coming to Jesus. In Matthew 11:28 Jesus tells us very simply, " Come to me...and I will give you rest." Oswald Chambers writes, "If we will come to Him, asking Him to produce Christ-awareness in us, He always will do it, until we fully learn to abide in Him." It is by coming to Jesus that we become less aware of ourselves and more aware of Jesus in our lives, and when we are more aware of Jesus in our lives, we are also more aware of the promises of God which are fulfilled and guaranteed in our lives because of Jesus (2 Corinthians 1:20). It is the promises of God which will allow us, in this time of fruit ripening, to enjoy the season despite what is going on around us, trusting that our lives will indeed yield fruit if we remain obedient to Jesus and abide in Him. God promises us that, "...He who has begun a good work in you will complete it..." (Philippians 1:6) and, "...may the God of peace make you complete in every good work to do His will, working in you what is well pleasing in His sight, through Jesus Christ..." (Hebrews 13:20-21). Go to Jesus, and allow Him to replace the turmoil of your self-awareness with the rest of His Christ-awareness and then enjoy that rest as He completes the ripening of your fruit which He has set in your life.

Remember

We are also to be obedient in remembering God's faithfulness. During this time, when God increases our awareness of His presence again and begins to establish the characteristics of Jesus in our lives, our state of emotional and even physical well-being improves drastically. However, it is this major improvement in our well-being, especially in comparison to that of Winter, when we are at risk of enjoying it all so much that we slowly start to forget that we now enjoy a healthier state of being because God remained faithful during our difficult seasons. We begin to forget that it was only by His grace and His mighty hand that we were brought into this new season of joy and growth (Deuteronomy 8:18). As a result, we forget to remain obedient to what God's word still commands. This warning comes to us out of the book of Deuteronomy. Moses told the Israelites to make sure that after entering the promised land, which God led them to (Deuteronomy 8:2), and after being nourished and fully satisfied by God's blessing in that land, they were to praise God and give Him thanks (Deuteronomy 8:10). With that instruction Moses also gave them a warning to be careful not to get so distracted with the blessing of the promised land that they would end up forgetting about God and His faithfulness which brought them into the land to begin with (Deuteronomy 8:11). This instruction and warning, given to us by God through the book of Deuteronomy, is perfectly applicable to the season we find ourselves in now. For we are always, as long as we are not yet resurrected and therefore remain in our earthly bodies, prone to being distracted by the blessings of God while ignoring God Himself as the source of our blessing. We need to guard our hearts to ensure that we do not become overly satisfied with God's blessings rather than focusing on God. To prevent this from happening, we must abound in thanksgiving and praise to God, "...singing and making melody in your heart to the Lord, giving thanks always for all things to God the Father in the name of our Lord Jesus Christ..." (Ephesians 5:19-20). A powerful way to remain in a state of praise and worship is by not constantly being on the lookout for God's blessings, and that includes not looking back on your own testimonies to be reminded of God's faithfulness (although at times that is indeed a wonderful way to remember God's faithfulness), but rather it is to gaze and meditate and wonder at the nature and characteristics of God and His eternal goodness and faithfulness. Charles H. Spurgeon writes, "Here is a standing reason for thanksgiving. Although we may not always be healthy, nor always prosperous, yet God is always good, and, therefore, there is always a sufficient argument for giving thanks unto Jehovah. That He is a good God essentially, that He cannot be otherwise than good, should be a fountain out of which the richest praises should perpetually flow." Let us then not forget the God who brought us into Spring and who has begun to display the likeness of His Son Jesus in our lives and let our desire to praise God be encouraged by the words of the prophet Isaiah, "O Lord, You are my God. I will exalt You, I will praise Your name, for you have done wonderful things..." (Isaiah 25:1). And let us too, like the psalmist, have a mouth that is filled with the praise and the glory of God all day long (Psalm 71:8).

Rejoice

The last practical application for Spring, is to be obedient in rejoicing in God. The Hebrew word for the verb "rejoices" is sus, and it means to be greatly happy and glad. From the verb sus also comes the noun sason, which means "joy and gladness". Therefore, to rejoice in God means to exhibit a behavior that is irresistibly joyful and entirely opposite to sadness or gloom. It means to live a life doing all things with an attitude characterized by this irresistible joy. The reason we are to be obedient to a lifestyle of rejoicing in God is because, in the first place, God is absolutely worthy of our rejoicing in Him. For although He is the everlasting God and the Creator of the ends of the earth (Isaiah 40:28), the One who measures oceans in His hands (Isaiah 40:12), the One who is God of gods, Lord of lords (Deuteronomy 10:17), the One who controls the clouds and makes lighting flash and the One who is "...Holy, holy, holy..." (Revelation 4:8), He still decided to make us the pinnacle of His creation and the object of His immeasurable and everlasting love (Psalm 8:4); a love displayed in the merciful act of sending His only Son to die for us, while we were still sinners (Romans 5:8). That on its own, is reason enough to rejoice every day. And then, in the second place, we are to rejoice in God because, throughout the Bible, He commands us to do so. We see this first in the Psalms. "Let Israel rejoice in their Maker; let the children of Zion be joyful in their King" (Psalm 149:2). "Rejoice in the Lord, you righteous..."(Psalm 97:12)."Be glad in the Lord and rejoice..."(Psalm 32:11). And again, "Oh, let the nations be glad and sing for joy..."(Psalm 67:4) And then God even commands nature, which He has created, to rejoice. "Let the heavens rejoice, and let the earth be glad..." (Psalm 96:11). And then we read the Gospels and Jesus is commanding us to "Rejoice and be exceedingly glad, for your reward is in heaven..." (Matthew 5:12). And again, "Rejoice in that day and leap for joy! For indeed your reward is great in heaven" (Luke 6:23). And then again, in the epistles, we are reminded of this command by Paul. "...rejoice in the Lord..." (Philippians 3:1). "Rejoice in the Lord always. Again I will say, rejoice!"(Philippians 4:4). It is clear that a life of obedient rejoicing is expected from a true Christian and follower of Jesus Christ. However, like all of God's commands, this obedient rejoicing is not to be pursued in a legalistic manner as a way to achieve righteousness with God. But rather, it is through a close fellowship with the Holy Spirit that we are enabled to rest in Jesus and to remember the faithfulness of God and it is through resting in Jesus and remembering God's faithfulness that our hearts are made glad and we desire to rejoice in God.

And so, having had our hearts tuned to the melody of heaven, we now continue along the path of faithfulness with joyful leaps and bounds and soon enough, we notice that Springtime is coming to an end. Below the soles of our dancing feet, the stones begin to warm and up ahead, in the distance, we see the path begin to glow as it floods with golden rays of glorious Summer sunshine. Our God has been faithful to us yet again, for Spring time is over and the Summer has now begun.

Chapter 4

Summer

Perfectly on time, God, from His mighty throne has now declared it to be Summer. The sun is granted a new schedule: warming the earth and extending the day. The cloudless, blue sky watches overhead as the vineyard begins to ripen in the soft, warm sunshine. The chirping birds play freely in the clear sunny air, landing only for a moment's rest and a quick cooling down in the shade of the bright green leaves of nearby branches. And, just before each day must end, the sun pauses for a moment at the horizon and turns back for one last look at his Master's perfect creation, smiles, and then scampers back to his heavenly home. And in the distance, a few dandelions float down in the sun's golden wake, seemingly longing to have just one more hour with their dear friend. Oh, how wonderful the Summer time is! It is a time where a sense of glory seems to hang in the air and God's faithfulness can be seen all around the vineyard, for God has indeed remained faithful; lovingly leading His vineyard through every season and bringing it safely into His glorious, bright Summer. In Summer, as we have seen with all the other seasons, there are natural principles which govern the vineyard. Before discussing these principles, I want to remind you, once more, to keep fresh in your memory the analogies I have brought before you thus far: that of the vineyard as the Christian life, the Gardener of that vineyard as Jesus Christ, and also the wonderful truth that God is sovereign over all the seasons.

Veraison

The first natural principle found in the vineyard in Summer, is Veraison. Veraison is originally a French term, now adopted into the English language, which describes the onset of the fruit-ripening process in the vineyard. The official definition of the word is, "change of colour of the grape berries". However, the definition provided does not honour the true intricacies which characterize the process. Veraison, beyond merely changing the colour of the grapes, is a complex process that transforms the hard, acidic, green berries that formed during "fruit-set" in Spring, into the soft, sweet, beautifully-coloured grapes that will eventually be ripe and ready for harvest. The ripening which takes place during Veraison occurs through five essential actions. The first is when the hard green berries soften. This softening takes place when the rigid cell walls of the berries begin to loosen as a result of a decrease in its turgor pressure (the force inside the cell pushing the internal contents against the cell wall). The second is the loosening of the cell walls so that the berries can begin to expand. This expansion takes place due to an increased flow of water into the berry. It is this flow of water into the berry which will be the key factor in the successful ripening of the berry. If the berry is to be fully ripe at harvest time, its composition must be at least 70% water. The third action is the accumulation of sugar in the berry. This happens when the Phloem (the artery-like structure which transports nutrients) begins to supply the berries with a large amount of sucrose, a type of sugar produced in the Chloroplast. The fourth action which occurs, is the decrease of the acidity levels of the berries. This decrease in acidity is mostly due to a large amount of malic acid which is absorbed and broken down as a source of energy for the grape cells. And finally, the fifth action which takes place during Veraison, is the establishing of the grape colours. The colours of the grapes are determined by the function of chlorophyll and anthocyanins. In red grapes, the chlorophyll which contains the green pigment that gives most of nature its green colour, is broken down and is simultaneously replaced with anthocyanins, which give the grape its red hue. In green grapes, the chlorophyll is not broken down and the anthocyanins are never produced. This allows the green grapes to keep their green shades. It is then these five processes: berry softening, berry expansion, sugar accumulation, acid decrease and colour formation which characterize the incredibly important process of Veraison. This process, under the watchful eye and meticulous care of the gardener, will ensure that the fruit which the vineyard yields in Summer is soft, sweet, beautiful and ripe for the day when the vineyard owner reaps his glorious harvest.

Harvest

The second natural principle that takes place in the vineyard during Summer time is the harvest. This is the final, and for the grapes, long-awaited event that takes place in the vineyard. It is the time when the grapes that have been so lovingly cared for by the gardener and which have grown and ripened into sweet fruit, are finally picked and brought into the storehouse. It is the fulfillment of what the vineyard owner planned from the beginning, and it is the moment that honours the loving care the gardener showed toward the owner's vineyard. Harvest is a wonderful time of celebration, where the fruit of the vine finally comes in and not a single grape on the vine is left behind. The instruction that the gardener gives to his labourers is clear. They are to pick every grape and bring it to the storehouse. Not one grape will remain on the vine. Although some grapes seem to be barely hanging on, although some grapes seem to have been damaged by the sun and although some grapes seem to not have grown to their full potential, they are all harvested. The vineyard owner has measured out the perfect yield for his harvest and he knows that each grape found on the vine during harvest, is part of that intended yield.

Having for the last time laid a foundation of natural principles, we are now ready to discover the final two spiritual considerations which the vineyard has to offer us. But before we do that, let us remember that we have not explored and unpacked these principles of nature for the mere acquisition of new knowledge. We have looked to the principles of nature with a hope that God would illuminate the spiritual truths found therein. Creation belongs to God (Psalm 24:1) and, therefore, there is nothing in nature which is separate from God. "For since the creation of the world His invisible attributes are clearly seen, being understood by the things that are made, even His eternal power and Godhead, so that they are without excuse..." (Romans 1:20). There is always something about God which we can discover by looking to nature. Charles H. Spurgeon writes, "The world is but the materializing of God's thoughts; for the world is a thought in God's eye. He made it first from a thought that came from His own mighty mind, and everything in the majestic temple that He has made, has a meaning." Let us then look to each natural principle found in Summer with the faith that God has indeed hidden therein glorious spiritual meaning.

Spiritual Conclusion 1

The first spiritual consideration that we can deduce from Summer, is found in Veraison, and it is the Holy process of sanctification. For a Christian, sanctification can be described as the process through which our spiritual fruit is renewed toward the likeness of Jesus Christ. Although the word ripening is well-suited to describe the process of Veraison in the vineyard, the word renewing is better suited to describe the process of sanctification in the life of a Christian. Sanctification is a renewing of one's life, by the power of the Holy Spirit, into the holiness of Jesus Christ.

Sanctification

Before we dive deeper into this process of sanctification, it is important to first clearly understand the two words that I will use to describe sanctification. They are: renewing and holy. The original word for renewing, used in the Bible, is the Greek word anakainos and the word suggests a restoration or a transformation. In his letter to Titus, Paul stresses that this process of restoration or transformation is a process that only takes place by the Holy Spirit (Titus 3:5). It can be said that renewing is the transformation work of the Holy Spirit. The word holy, used in the Bible, is the Hebrew word qadosh and it means to be sacred, pure and separated from anything that defiles that purity. We can now use this broader understanding of these two words to expand on our initial definition of sanctification by saying that sanctification is the process whereby our lives become sacred and pure (holy) through the transformation (renewing) work of the Holy Spirit. Not only does the Bible tell us what sanctification is, it also gives us an example of someone who was perfectly sanctified. Jesus tells us that He was sanctified (hagiazo) by God and then sent into the world (John 10:36). That is to say that God made Jesus (the human being) gloriously sacred and perfectly pure. In John 17:19 Jesus says, "...for their sakes I sanctify Myself, that they also may be sanctified...." Jesus, as the first and the only one perfectly complete in His sanctification, is our model of sanctification. A simple and practical definition of sanctification is, to become more like Jesus.

Now that we know what sanctification means and we know that sanctification is found in Jesus Christ. What remains to be answered is why we need to be sanctified and how we become sanctified. Christians need to be sanctified because sanctification is the will of God for our lives. We know this because on two occasions the Bible tells us this. In 1 Thessalonians 4:3 it says very clearly, "For this is the will of God, your sanctification..." and in Leviticus 11:44 God says, "For I am the Lord your God. You shall therefore consecrate yourselves, and you shall be holy; for I am holy...." Peter also reminds us of this in 1 Peter 1:16 when he tells us, "...you also be holy in all your conduct, because it is written, 'be holy, for I am holy." It is very clear then that God intends for us to be sanctified. How we become sanctified, must begin with the One who commands our sanctification: God. In 1 Thessalonians 5:23 Paul's final prayer is, "May the God of peace Himself sanctify you completely..." and in Leviticus 20:8 God says, "...I am the Lord who sanctifies you." Although our sanctification is God's desire for our lives, He did not separate Himself from our sanctification. Instead, God places Himself directly in our sanctification, saying that He will sanctify us. However, despite the fact that God is the One who sanctifies us, there is still a responsibility given to us to ensure that sanctification takes place. To understand this we must look at Leviticus 20:8 as well as Leviticus 20:7. By looking at both verses together, we see that God's promise of sanctification has a condition that we must obey. In Leviticus 20:7 God says, "Consecrate yourselves, and be holy, for I am the Lord your God." In Leviticus 20:8 God says, "And you shall keep My statutes, and perform them: I am the Lord who sanctifies you." Therefore the promise God makes in verse 8 to sanctify us, will only happen if we obey the command in verse 7, which tells us to consecrate ourselves. In other words, even though God is completely sovereign in our sanctification, it is still our responsibility to ensure that we are sanctified. Therefore, the answer to our question of how we are sanctified then has two parts. First, it is that we are indeed sanctified by God. That is to say, because God offered Jesus as the perfect atonement for our sins, and through our faith we accept Jesus as our Lord and Saviour, we are given the free opportunity to share in the sanctification of Jesus and to be made holy like He is. The second part of our answer is that we get to experience that sanctification which God offers through Jesus, by our obedience of consecration. So then, although our sanctification is ultimately the work of God, we need to display in our lives the evidence of that sanctification taking place in order that it may be perfected. And, we are to display that evidence every day. This is done by asking the Holy Spirit to transform us daily into the likeness of Jesus. It is done by drawing from God's new mercies and His never-ending love for us (Lamentation 3:22-23). It is done daily by asking the Holy Spirit to constantly remind us that we have crucified our former passions and desires (Galatians 5:24) and by asking the Holy Spirit to help us think only of things which are true, noble, just, pure, lovely, of good report, of virtue and praiseworthy (Philippians 4:8). Although it is a lifestyle of consistent daily consecration, it is important to realize that it is not a lifestyle of religious slavery. It is simply a sincere and consistent effort of the will to remain guided by the transforming power of the Holy Spirit. Living a life that is guided daily by the Holy Spirit, is not a life suffocated by rigidness or repression, but one to be enjoyed with a sense of freedom. For "...the Lord is the Spirit; and where the Spirit of the Lord is, there is liberty" (2 Corinthians 3:17).

Spiritual Conclusion 2

The second spiritual consideration that we can deduce from Summer is found in the harvest. For the Christian, this is the glorious event that our entire faith-filled life has built up to. It is that great day when we will see Jesus, the Son of Man, returning to earth on the clouds of heaven with power and great glory (Matthew 24:30). The day when Jesus "...will send His angels with a great sound of a trumpet, and they will gather together His elect..."(Matthew 24:31). It is the great day when we will finally finish our race on earth and be taken to our heavenly home to spend all of eternity in the presence of Jesus. However, we do not know when this great harvest will be. For Jesus said, "...of that day and hour no one knows, not even the angels in heaven, nor the Son, but only the Father" (Mark 13:32). But the day is indeed coming, and when that day does arrive there will not be a single person on the planet who is not a witness to this magnificent event. From the most faithful saints of Jesus, to the most determined deniers of Christ, "...every eye will see Him..." (Revelation 1:7). For the return of Jesus will be actual, personal and visible. And although we are now waiting, we must remember that this day will come suddenly, as a thief comes in the night (2 Peter 3:9,10). And the Bible tells us that it is already fast approaching. "But the end of all things is at hand..." (1 Peter 4:7). "Behold, I am coming quickly..." (Revelation 22:7). "...The Lord is at hand" (Philippians 4:5). And "...the coming of the Lord is at hand" (James 5:8). God is not delaying His return, therefore, we should not slack off in our service to Him. We must be faithful and continue the service of the Lord, confident that when He does return, He will find us busy doing the work He instructed us to do (Matthew 24:46). When Jesus returns, He is bringing with Him His reward, and He will give to each of us according to our work (Revelation 22:12). Therefore, let our behaviour as we wait be disciplined, and let us be watchful in prayer (1 Peter 4:7). Let us be obedient and keep the words of the prophecy of the Bible (Revelation 22:7). Let our character always be fair and considerate of others (Philippians 4:5). As God's chosen children, we need not doubt whether Jesus will gather us in, for the true followers of Jesus Christ will never perish and the devil will never snatch them out of the harvest basket (John 10:28). The emotional state that you are found in, will not determine whether you are brought in. The only prerequisite of being brought in at the harvest is that you are found still connected to the vine. And if you are indeed a true, spiritual follower of Jesus Christ, you will always be kept on the vine by the Holy Spirit who has sealed you until the day of Christ's return (Ephesians 4:30). Therefore, let your work not be to ensure that you are found on the vine on that glorious day, but rather let your work be done simply to glorify the incomprehensible mercy and love of God, who has ensured with His covenant promise that you will indeed be found on the vine. Let your work be done out of humble thanksgiving to God, who ensures that nothing can sever your life from the vine of Jesus Christ. "...neither death nor life, nor angels nor principalities nor powers, nor things present nor things to come, nor height nor depth, nor any other created thing, shall be able to separate us from the love of God which is in Christ Jesus our Lord" (Romans 8:38-39). Although your health may fail you or your friends depart from you, or your finances dry up, or your motivations become clouded, or your pride cripple you, or your good intentions run away from you - Jesus Christ, the Lord your God, will never leave you nor forsake you (Deuteronomy 31:6). If you are indeed a true follower of Jesus Christ; your life will never be separated from God. You will never perish and Jesus Christ will gather you into heaven's eternity, on that great day of harvest.

Practical Applications

Before we conclude this chapter, and with it the conclusion of our journey through the vineyard; I would like to share two practical applications that I believe will be of use to the Christians who find themselves in a spiritual Summer.

A Life of Repentance

The first practical application is that of living a life of daily repentance. As Christians who have been justified by the perfect sacrifice of Jesus Christ, we do not have a free pass to live a life of sin. As Paul writes in his letter to the Romans: "What then? Shall we sin, because we are not under the law but under grace? Certainly not!" (Romans 6:15). Instead, we are to live a life motivated by what Christ has done for us on the cross, and we should live according to what is written in 2 Corinthians 7:1 which says, "...let us cleanse ourselves from all filthiness of the flesh and the spirit, perfecting holiness in the fear of God." "For God did not call us to uncleanness, but in holiness" (1 Thessalonians 4:7). The way to perfecting our holiness is through living a life that reflects true repentance. The Greek word used for repentance in the Bible is metanoeo, and it means to make a determined decision that results in a change of mind. And for Christians it is a determined and deeply heartfelt decision to ask God for forgiveness of our sins and to help us turn away from that which is inhibiting our sanctification. It means to ask God for forgiveness for any area where we have failed to obey what He has commanded us to do. It may mean asking God to forgive the times when we have not loved Him with our entire life (Matthew 22:37). It may mean asking God to forgive the times when we complained and grumbled at doing things for Him or for other people (Matthew 22:39). It may also mean asking God for forgiveness for the times when we worried and put the cares of our heart above the capability of His might (Matthew 6:25). Whatever it is that we ask God for forgiveness in, it is important to realize that it should not be a formal request made to God out of feelings of guilt or shame that instinctively rise up after we have done things that we shouldn't have. Rather, it should be a sincere and grievous plea for God to forgive us of falling short of living a life worthy of the sacrifice of Jesus Christ, for God does not forgive us because He sympathizes with our feelings of guilt or regret, but rather because of Jesus who took all the punishment for us when He died on the cross. God does not want a formal gesture of forgiveness that involves a religious sacrifice as much as He wants "...a broken and contrite heart..."(Psalm 51:17), for God loves our honest and sincere plea for forgiveness, because that kind of true repentance is an indication that we have an understanding of the magnificence of the atonement of Jesus Christ. This kind of true repentance will come about through the conviction of the Holy Spirit. Jesus said that when the Holy Spirit came He would convict us (John 16:8), and this conviction is what produces in us a true sorrow. However, we do not create on our own ability this broken and contrite heart that God wants in our forgiveness, nor is it something that we can force or fake. Instead, we are to ask God for it, for true repentance is a gift that God grants us (2 Timothy 2:25). Therefore let us ask God to reveal to us where we are sinning in our lives, and let us ask God to grant us the Holy Spirit's conviction and the wonderful gift of true repentance. God is gracious and merciful, slow to anger and of great kindness (Joel 2:13) and "if we confess our sins, He is faithful and just to forgive us our sins and to cleanse us from all unrighteousness" (1 John 1:9). Although our God is indeed a merciful God, we must clearly understand that a true Christian will not live a life of perpetual sinning. If you are truly saved, then you will not want to sin, and you will be convicted by the gentle nudges of the Holy Spirit, for the Kingdom of God is not one that the unrighteous will inherit (1 Corinthians 6:9).

Pursue Jesus Christ

The second, and final practical application that I would like to present to you is that of living a life of consistently pursuing Jesus Christ. That is living a life of daily declaring and making Jesus Christ your ultimate and supreme treasure. In Philippians 3:12 Paul writes, "Not that I have already attained, or I am already perfected; but I press on, that I may lay hold of that for which Christ Jesus has also laid hold of me." What Paul is saying is that even though he has not made it to the end of his faith journey and he is not yet in a perfect relationship with Jesus, he continues his race and pursuit of that perfect relationship because that is the very thing for which Jesus Christ laid hold of him. He is not holding on and continuing because his eternal safety rests in the tightness of his grip and his ability to keep going, but rather he is holding on and pursuing Jesus because Jesus has already taken hold of him. It is the grip of Jesus that keeps Paul going, not the other way round. Paul does not press on to prove to God that he is worthy of the heavenly call, but rather he presses on to honour the faithfulness and worth of Jesus, who has already declared Paul worthy in Him. Our lives are to be lived in the same way; continually pressing on to take hold of that for which Jesus Christ has already taken hold of us, and the way to do that is through pursuing a deeper relationship with Jesus Christ. In Philippians 3:7,8 Paul writes, "But what things were gain to me, these I have counted loss for Christ. Yet indeed I also count all things loss for the excellence of the knowledge of Christ Jesus my Lord, for whom I have suffered the loss of all things, and count them as rubbish, that I may gain Christ." Although Paul made many mistakes in his life, which included persecuting innocent Christians, and now found himself trapped behind bars in a prison cell in Rome, nothing could keep him from pursuing Jesus. He realized that despite everything that had happened in his life and despite everything that would happen in his life, everything was worthless in comparison to knowing, enjoying and obeying Jesus Christ. That was the source of his deepest and most honest joy. And so too everything in our lives must be made secondary to knowing Jesus deeper. Our dreams, our desires, our jobs, our money, our houses, our health and even our friends should all be worthless in comparison to our relationship with Jesus. If we do indeed count Jesus as our supreme treasure and we seek Him honestly, God promises that we will find Him, for in Deuteronomy 4:29 it says, "...seek the Lord your God, and you will find Him if you seek Him with all your heart and with all your soul." And even in this, we can ask God to help us know the value of Jesus. We should therefore pray, "...satisfy us early with your mercy, that we may rejoice and be glad all our days" (Psalm 90:14), and also, "incline my heart to Your testimonies, and not to covetousness. Turn away my eyes from worthless things, and revive me in your way" (Psalm 119:36,37). Let us press on, and make God the supreme treasure of our lives, for there is no greater honour, no greater joy and no greater satisfaction than that of truly knowing Jesus Christ.

And so, our journey through the vineyard has come to an end. We have walked, stumbled, skipped and run along the glorious path of faithfulness, seeing the vineyard transform through the four seasons. In Autumn we saw how the vineyard experienced a necessary transition from lush and bright green to bare and golden brown. In Winter we experienced the silence of the vineyard in the perilous cold and with it, its branches being cut and shaped by the meticulous gardener. And then, in Spring, we saw the leaves return and the flowers begin to blossom and the first fruits begin to establish themselves on the branch. And finally, in Summer, we saw the sweet fruit ripen to perfection and the vineyard owner declaring the harvest ready and eventually bringing in his precious fruit. It has been a wonderful journey, and the path that we travelled along has indeed reached a glorious destination. Now we can see how the vineyard has been absolutely dependent on the vine and the care of the gardener and under the mercy and direction of God's weather. It is, however, important to note that although the natural vineyard experiences a cycle from Autumn to Summer in the space of a year, the Christian life is often a lot different. God may take you through many seasons in a very short time, possibly a few weeks, but He may also take you through these seasons over the period of many years. Although God's natural harvest happens in the time of a year, God's spiritual harvest does not meet any time frame that we know or can understand. However, the principle of His harvest is still sure and, therefore, if you continue to do as the branches of the vineyard do and abide on the vine throughout each season, your life will indeed continue to yield fruit each Summer, until the day when God eventually declares His harvest. And so, having equipped ourselves with the natural as well as spiritual knowledge of God's vineyard, we now have with us a strong foundation to securely answer the age-old question, "What is my purpose?", and in our case as Christians, What is my Divine Purpose?

DIVINE PURPOSE

Chapter 5

Our Divine Purpose

There can only be one true origin of our life purpose, for truth is absolutely exclusive. There is no right or left when it comes to truth, there is only right or wrong. It is my belief that the only origin of humanity's purpose is the three in one God of the Christian faith: the Father, the Son and the Holy Spirit. And the Bible is filled with scripture affirming this truth. "...the Lord Himself is God, there is none other besides Him" (Deuteronomy 4:35). "...the Lord is God; there is no other" (1 Kings 8:60). "...For I am God, there is no other; I am God, and there is none like me" (Isaiah 46:9). "...there is one God, and there is no other but He" (Mark 12:32). And it is only by knowing this one true God and Jesus Christ whom He sent, that we will be able to live according to the true purpose of life, and therefore have eternal life (John 17:3). Therefore to understand what our Divine Purpose is, is simply to know what God's purpose for making us was. For if we live according to His purpose for creating us, then we will be living according to our Divine Purpose.

In the pages to follow I will explain firstly what God's purpose was for creating mankind, and then having that knowledge I will attempt to show you that our

Divine Purpose is simply to live a life that always seeks, abides, and obeys Jesus Christ, for it is through perpetually seeking, abiding and obeying Jesus, that we end up fulfilling God's ultimate purpose.

The prophet Isaiah writes, "Everyone who is called by My name, who I have created for My glory; I have formed him, yes, I have made him" (Isaiah 43:7). This verse tells us three things: it tells us that God created us. It tells us that God called us to Him, and it tells us that God created us and called us to Him for His glory. God's purpose for creating us is to bring Him glory. The Hebrew word used for glory is chabod, and it means splendour, magnificence, power, riches, excellence and honour. John Piper writes, "God's glory is the perfect harmony of all His attributes into one infinitely beautiful and personal being." God, in His infinite beauty, created us so that His splendour, magnificence, power, riches, excellence and honour of His personal being would be made known throughout the earth by our declaring it. Therefore, everything we do in life is to be done in a way that declares and makes known His glory throughout the world (1 Corinthians 10:31). However, I believe many Christians are mistakenly assuming that they need to be doing a particular task or have a particular career in order to properly bring God glory and, as a result, many Christians are striving and losing their peace in pursuit of what that one thing is. Some Christians are even delaying a life of discipleship simply because they have not yet been shown where they should be disciples. And yes, God indeed has certain places where He wants you to do His will, and He will definitely reveal to you in His perfect time where that is. However, Jesus told us to "seek first the Kingdom of God and His righteousness, and all these things shall be added to you" (Matthew 6:33). I believe that many are waiting for things to be added to them, but they are not first seeking the Kingdom. Many are ready to be disciples poured out in magnificent ways for the Kingdom, but they are not ready to first do the very simple thing of seeking Jesus. As a result, many Christians are delaying the chance to bring God glory. To those Christians I would like to say that living a life that brings God glory is not found in a particular task or career. You do not need to be painstakingly waiting for that to be a true disciple of Christ. If you do the very simple act of seeking, abiding and obeying Jesus, then He will guide you into all the things that will bring God glory. Giving God glory is not only found in the significant duties, but also, in as much splendour, God's glory is found in the seemingly insignificant tasks of life. We can give God as much glory on the preaching platform as we do while making our bed in the morning. To glorify God is about the sincerity of the heart, more than it is about the might of our hands.

Seek

The Bible tells us that we are to "seek the Lord and His strength; seek His face evermore" (Psalm 105:4). If we do this, then we will indeed find Him (1 Chronicles 28:9). Although God is omnipresent and His presence is always with everything, and His promise is also to be with us always until the very end (Matthew 28:20), we are not always aware of His presence. It's as if, at times, we have our spiritual eyes closed to the presence of God. And so, to seek God does not mean to look for Him as if He were missing. The Hebrew word used for seek is baqash, which means to diligently look for God and to keep doing that until you find Him. A life of seeking God, therefore, means to continually be on the lookout for Him in everything we do and everywhere we go. It means to look for God in His Word, for there we will find His wisdom, His commands, His character and His plan of redemption. It means to look for God in the godly people around us. There we will find His kindness in a hug, His compassion in a friend's sympathy, His joy in a smile and His help. It means to look for God's character expressed in nature. There we will find His power in the roar of the ocean, His beauty in a summer sunset, His creativity in the colours of the rainbow and His gentleness in a passing butterfly. God is truly everywhere and if we seek Him humbly and with faith in everything we do and everywhere we go, we will find Him, because He is faithful to His word. We must ask the Holy Spirit to remove from our eyes the worldly veil that we so often look through and to help us see things as they are meant to be seen. It is only with a heavenly perspective that we start to see the things of heaven. We must not fall into the trap of chasing after the materialistic things of this world, for they cannot come close to the surpassing worth of finding Jesus Christ. Instead, we should "seek first the kingdom of God and His righteousness, and all these things will be added to us" (Matthew 6:33). Although these added things will never come close to the satisfaction of knowing Jesus, they are gifts given to us by our loving and generous Father; rewards for seeking Him with an honest and sincere heart, not for a desire of the gifts, but for a desire for Him.

Abide

In John 15:4 Jesus tells us, "Abide in Me, and I in you. As the branch cannot bear fruit of itself, unless it abides in the vine, neither can you, unless you abide in me." We have seen just how true this is in the natural vineyard, and we know just how true it is for us as Christians. So how exactly do we abide in Jesus Christ? In John 15:10 Jesus gives us the answer. He says, "if you keep my commandments, you will abide in My love, just as I have kept My Father's commandments and abide in His love." To abide in Jesus simply means to keep His commandments and the commandments Jesus gave us are found in Matthew 22:37-39 which says, " ...you shall love the Lord your God with all your heart, with all your soul and with all your mind. This is the first and the greatest commandment. And the second is like it: 'You shall love your neighbour as yourself." To abide in Jesus Christ, therefore, requires us to keep these two commandments. The first requires us to love Jesus with all our heart, soul and mind. The Hebrew word used for heart is leb, and it refers to our deepest thoughts and innermost feelings. Our love for Jesus needs to be at the very foundation of everything we think and feel. There should not be a thought or feeling that surpasses the thoughts and feelings of our love for Jesus Christ. The Hebrew word for soul is nephesh, and it refers to our entire being and person. We are, therefore, also commanded to love God with every part of who we are. Our entire personality should love God. We are to love God within our creativity, our physical activity and even our sense of humour. The Greek word used for mind is dianoia, and it refers to our understanding and perception. We are, therefore, also commanded to love God with our intellectual ability. This means that we are to love God in our reasoning and understanding of Him. The second commandment we need to keep in order to abide in Jesus is to love our neighbour like ourselves. This does not mean that we first need to love ourselves and have a good self-esteem in order to love our neighbours, but rather it means that we are to love others in the same way that we would want to be loved. It means to do unto others what we would want them to do unto us (Matthew 7:12). It means we are to be concerned with other people's happiness as much as with our own. It means to be dedicated to alleviating the suffering of others as much as we are dedicated to alleviating our own. To abide in Jesus Christ is not always easy, but it is necessary if our lives are to bear the fruit that will glorify God. Therefore, make the determined effort every day to abide in Jesus Christ. Ask the Holy Spirit to pour out the love of God into your heart every day (Romans 5:5), so that you will know that you are loved by God. Then, you will be able to love Him fully and you will overflow with His love for your neighbours.

Obey

The final way in which our lives can bring God glory, is by living a life of obedience to Jesus Christ. The Greek word for obedience is hupakoe, which means to be attentive to hearing and to listen with compliance and submission. The word was mostly used for servants who would be diligently attentive to the requirements of their master. In the same way then we, as servants of Jesus Christ, are to diligently listen to what He commands us to do and to boldly carry out His instructions. In Romans 5:19 Paul writes, "For as by one man's disobedience many were made sinners, so also by one man's obedience many will be made righteous." Adam disobeyed God's voice in the beginning and the consequence of this resulted in the entire human race being born into sin, and made guilty before God. Disobeying essentially means to rebel against God and reject His plan. The reason we so often end up disobeying God is twofold. Firstly, we disobey God's request because we are afraid of the worldly consequence of that obedience. We become fearful about what people might say about us, or afraid of how people will respond to us (1 Samuel 15:24). We regard the worldly consequence of our obedience as more important than the heavenly consequence of our disobedience. Secondly, we disobey God's request because we think there might be a better or different way of doing things. We rely on our own wisdom and we put our trust in our own understanding. We foolishly think that we are wiser than God. In both instances we exalt these rebellious thoughts above the knowledge of God, thus we are committing idolatry. If we are to obey God then, we need to ensure that we take these rebellious thoughts captive and submit them in obedience to Jesus Christ (2 Corinthians 10:5). We need to ensure that the thoughts which challenge the requests of God, and attempt to lure us into disobedience, are destroyed. How do we do this? We do this by drawing on the mighty power of God, for in 2 Corinthians 10:4 it says, "...the weapons of our warfare are not carnal but mighty in God...." Therefore, although it is so often the thoughts of our own flesh which attempt to exalt themselves above the knowledge of God, our tools for conquering those fleshly thoughts are not of the flesh, but from the mighty power of God. So, whenever we are tempted with thoughts that rebel against the requests of God, we are to ask the Holy Spirit to help us take those thoughts captive. Often we have thoughts that make us eager to do work for the Lord. Very often these thoughts are from our flesh too and they are more concerned with sacrifice than obedience. However, to God, our obedience is far better than our sacrifice (1 Samuel 15:22) and to listen to God and to do what we are told, is much better than doing many things out of our own desires and strength. Oswald

Chambers writes, "...true determination and zeal are found in obeying God, not in the inclination to serve Him that arises from our own undisciplined nature." We must live lives of consistent obedience to the requests of God, not being concerned with the outcome of that obedience but rather dedicated only to the process of being obedient. It is through the process of faithful obedience that we exalt the knowledge and power of God above all other things and it is through that exalting that God is glorified.

Our Divine Purpose, as Christians, is simply to live a life of daily seeking, abiding and obeying our Lord Jesus Christ. Let us not complicate our duty as Christians and get lost in the pursuit of self-satisfying sacrificial service. Instead, let us pursue the very simple Gospel for what it is - Jesus Christ Himself. Let us look for Jesus in everything, let us love Jesus deeply and let us listen diligently to His voice. It is those who earnestly look for Jesus, who truly love Him and who obediently listen to Him each day, who are worthy of being called His disciples, and it is His disciples that bring Him the greatest glory, and who ultimately live within the purpose for which we were all created!

Chapter 6

The Vineyard

Earlier in the book I said that we have a supernatural enemy whose aim is to hurt us, deceive us, distract us and to destroy anything in our lives that puts the glory of God on display. The Bible calls Him the devil and Satan (Revelation 12:9) and he "...walks about like a roaring lion, seeking whom he may devour" (1 Peter 5:8). This enemy is our greatest foe and, as Christians, we are in day-in and day-out spiritual warfare with him. Therefore, like soldiers on a battlefield, we are to be armed at all times and ready for combat. We are to be on guard and ready to "fight the good fight of faith..." (1 Timothy 6:12) the moment the enemy launches an attack. To do so, we must start each day fully equipped in our battle armour.

Armour of God

In Ephesians 6:13-18 we are told more about this battle armour: "...take up the whole armour of God, that you may be able to withstand in the evil day...stand therefore having girded your waist with truth, having put on the breastplate of righteousness, and having shod your feet with the preparation of the gospel of peace; above all things, taking the shield of faith with which you will be able to quench the fiery darts of the wicked one. And take the helmet of salvation, and the sword of the Spirit, which is the word of God…" From head to toe we are protected: a helmet of salvation, a breast-plate of righteousness, a shield of faith, a sword of the Spirit, a belt of truth and shoes of the gospel of peace. The way we dress ourselves in this armour each morning, is through prayer and supplication in the spirit. To put on the helmet of salvation means to pray for understanding that our faith in the death and resurrection of Jesus Christ assures us eternal life (John 3:16). It means to pray for the understanding that the devil will never be able to pluck us out of the hands of Jesus (John 10:28). It means to pray for understanding that God will deliver us from every evil work and preserve us until we make it to heaven (2 Timothy 4:18). It is through understanding and believing that we are indeed saved and kept by Jesus Christ, that we protect our thoughts from the lies of the devil which try to create worry, anxiety and fear in us. To put on the chest-plate of righteousness means to pray for the Holy Spirit to help us live in righteous obedience (Romans 14:17). Living in a way that is righteous, protects us from giving in to the temptations of the devil. To put on the shield of faith literally means to ask God to increase our faith in Him (Luke 17:5). It also means to read the word of God each morning so that our faith will increase. For "…faith comes by hearing and hearing by the word of God" (Romans 10:17). This faith is essential, for as J.C Ryle writes, "faith is the hinge on which victory turns. Success depends entirely on believing." To pick up the sword of the Spirit means to speak scripture back to the lies of our adversary, in the same way that Jesus did in the wilderness (Matthew 4:10). Scripture is the truth of God's Word and it has the power to rebuke the lies of the devil. To put on the belt of truth means to equip ourselves with the truth of God's word and God's promises. It means to ask God to remind us of our identity and our security in Christ, for to know who we are and whose we are, is to believe a truth that will allow us to be available for God's will. It is only within your identity in Christ that you can be of value to God's plan. The devil will attempt to corrupt how you identify yourself. He will attempt to deceive you into questioning the truth that you have been made exclusively, as either a man or a woman, in the image of God. He will attempt to corrupt the truth that you are a child of God and the object of His affection. Never forget that the devil is the father of lies, and there is no truth within him (John 8:44). So, if these lies start to come your way, then earnestly pray for God's truth to preserve you and for God's truth alone to define your identity as the man or the woman God created you to be, a child of God whom He chose and called into His family. Finally, we are to put on as shoes the gospel of peace, for in Romans 16:20 it says, "...the God of peace will crush Satan under your feet shortly...." Therefore, to put on the gospel shoes of peace means to ask God to help you believe and remember that one day His word will prevail, and that one day Satan will indeed be defeated. If we understand and believe this, then we can trample the attack of the enemy under the mighty and peaceful truth of the Gospel's victory. Having dressed ourselves each day in the mighty armour of God, we are ready to take to the battlefield and take ground for God's Kingdom.

This battle is not always easy, and many have been wounded while waging war with the enemy. Sadly, many of these wounded Christians have retreated and now hang back far from enemy lines, watching their fellow soldiers take ground on the front lines. For these soldiers of Christ I have a word of encouragement. Your Commander, Jesus Christ, has the authority and the power to bind up your wounds (Psalm 147:3) and to give you the strength (Isaiah 41:10) you need to keep fighting the good fight of faith. Therefore, turn to Jesus Christ, your Captain, the Commander of heaven's armies and ask Him for healing and He will give it to you. For the Bible says, "Heal me, O Lord, and I shall be healed..." (Jeremiah 17:14). And then finally, as we go to battle, we need not be afraid of anything that comes our way. No matter how fierce and intimidating our enemy is and no matter how many come up against us, we need not fear anything. The Bible tells us, "...do not be afraid of them, for the Lord your God is with you... to fight against the enemies, to save you" (Deuteronomy 20:3,4). We do not have to fight this battle in our own strength. All we need to do is "...position ourselves, stand still and see the salvation of the Lord..." (2 Chronicles 20:17), for the victory has already been claimed by Jesus Christ.

An Eternal Choice

Before we reach the end of this book, there is one last thing that I would like to share with you, and in particular with the men and woman who have read this book having never before heard the name Jesus Christ, or who have, but have never believed and surrendered to Him as the only King and Saviour of the world. Jesus Christ is the Son of God. He is the word of God. Before the foundation of the world was created, Jesus existed. He has existed for all eternity; from everlasting to everlasting is His existence. Over two-thousand years ago, Jesus, the word of God, became flesh and entered the world as a man. He was still fully God, but also fully man. His reason for coming was to set us free from sin and to save us from God's wrath. For, from the moment that Adam and Eve were deceived by the devil and rebelled against God's commands, the entire human race from that point forth was born into sin. The world and everything in it became corrupted by sin. And God, being perfect in righteousness and justice, could no longer have fellowship with us, because we were tainted with sin. The only way for us to be reunited with God was through an atoning sacrifice, and Jesus Christ was that sacrifice. Jesus Christ came to earth to die for our sins. His blood that was shed for us, has washed us clean of our sin. Therefore, when God looks to those who have been saved by the blood of Jesus, He no longer sees their iniquity, but rather He sees innocence and purity. God no longer needs to punish us for our sins, for Jesus took all of the punishment for us. Jesus literally died for us, so that we would not have to. He tasted death for us, so that we would not have to. But Jesus did not stay dead, instead God raised Jesus from the dead, and in so doing Jesus conquered death. Jesus has eternal life and the power and authority to offer eternal life to anyone. And Jesus offers that gift of forgiveness and eternal life to everyone. There is no person on the planet who cannot drink from this everlasting spring. For Jesus says, "...if anyone thirsts, let Him come to Me and drink" (John 7:37). Jesus Christ offers us all eternal life as a gift of love and mercy. If you believe in Jesus Christ as your Lord and Saviour, you will not perish but have everlasting life. You will not taste death, but you will reign in heaven with God forever. It is a gift; you have done nothing to deserve it, and you can do nothing to earn it. It is a gift given to us out of the abundant mercy, kindness and love of God. May your hearts be softened, and may you accept Jesus Christ as your Lord and Saviour and lay down your life completely, so that God can lead you into your Divine Purpose.

Epilogue

I read a quote in the introduction of David Pawson's book Unlocking the Bible that says, "certain authors, speaking of their works, say 'my book' ...they would do better to say 'our book'... because there is in them usually more of other people's than their own" (the original came from Blaise Pascal). And so, to what would no doubt have delighted Pascal, I am more than content to say that this is not my book, but rather our book; one that I share with several followers of Jesus Christ who have come before me. For, it is through their collective writings, which are so vast that I would not be able to read them all in a lifetime, that God has given me a greater understanding of what Jesus Christ did for us on the Cross. Therefore, to their obedience in writing for God's glory, honour is due. However, it remains the glorious reality that everything true which has ever been written on the Christian faith has its source in one man, Jesus Christ, and it is upon His shoulders alone that all the truths of Christianity stand. My hope is that this book has magnified His name and has pointed you in His direction, for Jesus Christ is indeed "...the Way, the Truth and the Life" (John 14:6).

Unto God be the Glory!

www.ingramcontent.com/pod-product-compliance
Lightning Source LLC
LaVergne TN
LVHW041234080426
835508LV00011B/1203